I firmly believe that great leaders lead in vulnerability. Nona gives us the type of vulnerability that allows us to know that success is possible no matter what your circumstances are. The stories in this book are a reflection of you and me. This is a book people need.

Lecrae, Grammy Award–winning
artist and bestselling author

To write a book such as this truly took a tremendous amount of courage and a deep passion for helping others overcome pain from past trauma. Nona Jones's transparency and insight into her most painful experiences will undoubtedly help readers overcome their darkest experiences so they can experience all the goodness and success that is waiting for them on the path to redemption and empowerment!

Laila Ali, author, TV host, champion boxer, and CEO

Nona Jones shows, in *Success from the Inside Out*, that God's grace is strong enough to lift us up when we have no strength left with which to stand. This book is not only for professionals but for anyone who needs freedom from their past to fully embrace their future.

Bishop T. D. Jakes, *New York Times* bestselling author, international speaker, senior pastor of The Potter's House of Dallas

In *Success from the Inside Out*, my dear friend Nona Jones opens up about the abuse she suffered in her childhood and how she turned tragedy into triumph. She helps others overcome their past traumas by providing tools that lead to a successful life. Nona's strength and story will inspire, motivate, and transform you!

DeVon Franklin, Hollywood producer and
New York Times bestselling author

Looking at Nona Jones, you would never have guessed that she grew up in so much pain and heartache, but in *Success from the Inside Out*, she shows us by example that God gives us beauty for ashes. This book is needed by the masses because so many people are allowing their futures to be stolen by past pain. I'm looking forward to seeing this book heal many.

Miles McPherson, bestselling author of *The Third Option* and senior pastor of The Rock, San Diego

We must all know each other's stories in order to realize that we are one. We can't judge people without knowing their true pain. In *Success from the Inside Out*, Nona's honest and transparent story helps heal all wounds and gives you hope.

Nely Galán, *New York Times* bestselling author of *Self Made*

Regardless of whether you've experienced the personal pain of sexual or physical abuse, Nona's story of overcoming is proof positive that with God's hope and grace we are much more than the sum of our experiences. God's redemptive power always beats the odds. *Success from the Inside Out* is a true inspiration!

Matt and Laurie Crouch, chairman and CEO of Trinity Broadcasting Network

A leader can be outwardly successful while internally suffering from their past. In *Success from the Inside Out*, Nona Jones delivers wise and practical teaching with raw honesty on how leaders can turn past pain into purpose. If you think you're "over it" but continue to struggle with private feelings of unworthiness, this book is for you.

Carey Nieuwhof, founding pastor of Connexus Church and author of *Didn't See It Coming*

What an incredible book! Nona Jones gets to the core of *true* success—not the shiny and shallow but the deep and meaningful—and shows us how to experience it. Don't miss out on this life-giving and powerful message.

Les Parrott, PhD, #1 *New York Times* bestselling author of *Love Like That*

SUCCESS *from the* INSIDE OUT

SUCCESS *from the*
INSIDE OUT

NONA JONES

ZONDERVAN

Success from the Inside Out
Copyright © 2020 by Nona Jones

Requests for information should be addressed to:
Zondervan, *3900 Sparks Dr. SE, Grand Rapids, Michigan 49546*

Zondervan titles may be purchased in bulk for educational, business, fundraising, or promotional use. For information, please email SpecialMarkets@Zondervan.com.

ISBN 978-0-310-35760-5 (hardcover)

ISBN 978-0-310-35763-6 (audio)

ISBN 978-0-310-35762-9 (ebook)

Cover design: Micah Kandros
Cover photo: James Schlefstein
Interior design: Denise Froehlich

Printed in the United States of America

19 20 21 22 23 LSC 10 9 8 7 6 5 4 3 2 1

In loving memory of D'Wayne Isaac Collins. Daddy, you were afraid I wouldn't remember you, but everything I've ever achieved is because of you. I love you and hope I've made you proud.

Foreword

Nona Jones is a gift to the kingdom of God, to you, and to me. Her life story is one that reminds us all that no matter how we start out in life, we can finish good. While we may not be able to rewrite our history, we can certainly change the narrative going forward. Nothing can hold us back from fulfilling the plans and purposes God has for our lives when we yield to him. Our lives redeemed by God can be an inspiration to others so that they can finish good too.

As a mother in the faith, I get so excited when I see young women like Nona—women who have overcome, who have true character and integrity, who are passionate to help others find the freedom that is found only in Christ. I am moved by her heart and inspired by her overcoming spirit.

I am so grateful for how she discovered—much like I did in my own life—that just because we might come from a background that is painful or difficult or where the odds are stacked against us, none of us have to accept a life of defeat.

In Romans 8:28 (CSB), the apostle Paul wrote, "We know that all things work together for the good of those who love God, who are called according to his purpose."

From the time Nona discovered God—from the time God drew her to himself—she loved him and began to live for him. Because of that, she learned the powerful truth that God is good, God does good, and God works all things together for her good—throughout every season of her life. It is from that core foundation that she discovered God's way of success and penned her journey.

Throughout the pages of *Success from the Inside Out*, Nona's faith will inspire you, and the biblical principles she has woven throughout her story will show you how you can be successful in every area of your life—in your educational pursuits, in your career, in your marriage, in your parenting, and in the destiny God has called you to pursue.

I appreciate how Nona makes the careful distinction that we're not to want just any kind of success, but we're to pursue what God calls *good* success. Through the words of Joshua 1:8 (ESV), God instructs us: "This Book of the Law shall not depart from your mouth, but you shall meditate on it day and night, so that you may be careful to do according to all that is written in it. For then you will make your way prosperous, and then you will have good success."

Nona is a powerful example of what it means to have *good* success, the kind of success we choose by believing God's Word over our past and by allowing it to transform us from the inside out. I believe in Nona because she lives what she has written, and she articulates it so well in the pages of this book. Dive into every chapter with your whole heart, and allow God to give you his *Success from the Inside Out!*

CHRISTINE CAINE, bestselling author,
founder of A21 & Propel Women

Contents

BEYOND
SURVIVING

Chapter 1

Surviving Isn't Enough

Warning: This chapter recounts memories of a traumatic event that may trigger painful memories in others who have survived sexual abuse. If you begin to feel anxious while reading the recollection, please skip to chapter 2.

"Please take me with you. I'll be good."

I was just settling into kindergarten when Mom got the call that her sister had passed away. She told me she had to go back home to New Jersey to attend the funeral. When I walked into my mother's room to find her packing her large gray suitcase, my little five-year-old heart ached to go with her. She never lifted her gaze to meet mine, but if she had only glanced in my direction, perhaps she would have caught a glimpse of the fear in my eyes.

"I don't have the money for another plane ticket, Nona. I'll be back after the funeral. It's only a few days."

"But . . . I . . . I'll be good. I won't ask for anything."

"Look. I said I can't afford to take you. Just stay here with Lee. You don't need to miss school anyway."

I didn't want her to leave me. But more importantly, I didn't want her to leave me . . . with him. Mom and Lee had been together only a couple of months when she let him move in with us, and it wasn't long after that things became toxic between the two of them. By the time her sister died, they had been together a little less than a year, but the constant fighting made it seem like an eternity.

Lee didn't have a job, but he got a monthly disability check from the government for being born with cerebral palsy. She invited him to move in with us because she figured that instead of him paying rent for an apartment, he could contribute that money to her mortgage. But the amount of money he got every month was apparently less than she expected, because they regularly argued about how little money he contributed to their living expenses.

Their fighting became a constant backdrop to my daily existence, with her calling him names and him yelling back at her in frustration, threatening to leave. She would back down after he told her he was leaving, but her frustration with him continued to mount until it started boiling over at me. She would become so enraged with him that she would hit me for any minor infraction—if I left a toy on the floor or didn't walk fast enough in a store or didn't make my bed.

I never knew what would set her off, so I became extra careful at home in an effort to not make her angry. But it didn't work. My attempts at perfection never measured up, and the only thing I knew for sure was that when Lee pulled her anger trigger, I became the verbal, emotional, and physical target.

One day, shortly after I started kindergarten, Lee cornered me in the family room while Mom was out running errands. He started tickling me under my arms and along my sides, making me laugh uncontrollably. I laughed so hard that I ended up on the floor, where he kept tickling me with one hand while using his other arm to hold me down. Once he had me pinned to the ground, his tickles started moving to my private parts. I told him to stop and wiggled my way out from under him. Once I got free, he said, "You know I was just playing with you. We were just having fun." I didn't think it was fun.

Another time when Mom wasn't home, he asked me for a hug. After I gave him a hug, he refused to let me go. He squeezed me tight against his body, too tight. I remember thinking it felt as though there were something in his pants. I was too young to understand. I fought to get out of his embrace, and he laughed as he let me go, calling me "feisty" as he walked away. I remember him calling me into the guest bedroom and pulling out a hidden stash of *Playboy* magazines to show me pictures of naked women. He said the women were pretty—"Pretty like you, Nona." I took one look at the lady on the page and immediately lowered my eyes. There was something dirty about it, so I stared at the floor until he finished talking.

Between my mom's and his arguing, the beatings from my mom, and Lee's regular attempts to touch me inappropriately, the chaos behind the closed doors of our house spilled out into my behavior in the classroom. I showed up to class both exhausted and hyper most days. I lost sleep many nights from staring at my closed bedroom door. I didn't know who would show up each night—Mom in a fit of rage or Lee in a fit of lust. Many nights I would wake to find Lee standing over me, feeling himself. Mom often told me I was a burden on her and that her life would be better if I hadn't been born, so I believed at a young age that my *own* life would be better if I hadn't been born. The seeds of suicidal thoughts were planted in me by my mother before I even had a vision for a future.

Not long into my first year of school, I had already been labeled a "problem child." I would talk back to my teacher if I didn't want to do something, and I didn't do my school-work because I couldn't focus. In response to my behavior at school, the teachers attempted to discipline me by making the classroom corner my permanent home. No one ever asked me why I was behaving the way I did. They just labeled me "disruptive" and "defiant." Nobody knew what I was battling at home. And no one cared enough to ask. At one point, my teachers told my mom that I showed signs of "mental retardation." They said I had difficulty learning as evidenced by my not doing my school work and that I needed remedial education. Mom had the school administer a learning assessment, and to everyone's surprise, I tested as gifted. This "problem child" certainly had a problem, but it wasn't learning.

The first night Mom was gone for her sister's funeral, I locked my bedroom door. I intrinsically knew I needed that barrier between me and Lee to be safe. But as I started to slip into sleep, I heard my doorknob turn, then click against the lock. It turned a few more times, then stopped. I pulled my blanket around me tighter, as if it could become a force field of protection, but I learned that night that a straightened wire hanger could pick the lock.

Scratch. Scratch. Scratch. Click.

Silence. Darkness. Then a soft stream of light poured into my room from the hallway as the door opened. I pulled my blanket up to my nose, attempting to fade into the darkness, but as Lee made his way through my door and into my bedroom, the soft glow of the night-light reflected in his eyes. He was staring straight at me, the way a predator stares at his prey. Because that's what he was. A predator. He walked straight to my bed and ripped the blanket from my tightened grasp.

He told me he knew I'd been wanting it. And that no one would ever know. That it would be our little secret.

I told him no and asked him to please stop.

He didn't listen.

Part of me died the night Lee stole my innocence. And to this day, the faint smell of beer on someone's breath often takes my mind back to that night.

When he finished, he told me, "You better never tell your mom, or she'll get rid of you. She doesn't want you anyway."

Lee didn't break only my body that night, *he broke my spirit.*

I didn't have any brothers or sisters. I didn't have any aunts or uncles or cousins living nearby. I was entirely alone, without anyone to turn to.

Maybe that's you too. Maybe you've faced a loss or

trauma or challenge by yourself, and the only power you've been able to muster is the power to simply get through it. Simply survive. Or maybe you *did* have people in your life who cared about you, but they simply missed the signs of what you were enduring. I understand that deeply and want you to know you are not alone. So many of us in this world are just putting one foot in front of the other every day, and we look around at the smiling faces of our friends, family, and coworkers and think no one else understands. Yet despite what it may look like, many people have been where you are, and even more people are still there. You are not alone.

Children are so innocent. They trust that the adults in their lives will protect them from harm. They assume the "big people" telling them what to do and what not to do have the best intentions. Innocence is a precious gift, and when parents and loved ones don't protect our innocence, they leave us exposed and vulnerable to the bad intentions of others. This is why I believe a parent's greatest responsibility is to cherish their child's vulnerability.

You may have experienced a deep hurt at the hands of a loved one and are still struggling to this day to regain the part of you that was lost. You survived the trauma, but now what?

> The only thing stronger than the power of trauma is the power we *reclaim* when we acknowledge trauma's effect on us.

I have come to believe that the only thing stronger than the power of trauma is the power we *reclaim* when we acknowledge trauma's effect on us. Surviving is only the beginning.

———∞∞∞———

When Mom came back home from the funeral, I was an entirely different child. Before she left, I talked nonstop. When she returned, I was quiet. I even avoided eye contact with her, afraid she would see in my eyes what had happened. In my little mind, it was my fault. I had done something wrong. I was afraid she would be angry with me for what had happened. For months afterward he abused me when she had to work late. Every time he finished, he would remind me that she would get rid of me if I ever told her what "we" did. But one night she took me to work with her, and something broke inside me as we drove back home.

As we drove back home in the middle of the night, I had a pit in my stomach. Little tears formed in the corners of my eyes. The thought of going back to that house with him in it sickened me. It was the first time in a long time that my mom and I were alone. I was six years old by then, and my first-grade teacher told my mom I was still being defiant at school. I had wanted to tell her what was happening to me so many times before, but because of Lee's threats, the thought of being taken away by strangers almost took my voice away. Almost.

"Lee touched me."

Silence.

". . . What?" she said, her voice shaking.

"Lee . . . touched me."

"Touched you how?" she asked.

"Down there. And it hurt."

"Show me how he did it," she asked, staring at the road without blinking.

When we arrived home, the house was dark except for the glow of light coming from their bedroom. I walked behind my mom as she set her purse on her bed. Lee was standing in front of their bathroom mirror, shaving. My mother silently went into her closet and pulled out the little wooden bat my father bought me as a baby, then she made her way toward the bathroom. I backed out of her room, and when I was just outside her bedroom door, I heard the first blow land.

Crack!

"What are you doing?" Lee screamed. "Stop! Wait! Stop! What are you doing?"

"You touched my daughter? *My* daughter?"

"No! No! I would never . . ."

Crack! Slam! Crash!

"I'm sorry! Wait! Please! I'm sorry!"

My mom emerged from her room breathing heavily, with a look of complete ferocity in her eyes. She walked past me to the kitchen and called the cops. After she hung up the phone, she walked back to the room, where she proceeded to curse him out between blows.

Despite the dysfunction and abuse, that night I felt as though my mom was my own personal superhero. My mom was Wonder Woman. Invincible. Strong. When the police arrived, they questioned my mom, and Lee admitted what he did. They took him away, and for the first night in months, I slept with my door wide open. I was safe.

I was brought in for questioning and was asked to describe what he had done to me as best I could with my six-year-old vocabulary. When the questioning was finished, the officers assured me I wouldn't have to worry about Lee hurting me again. But they never contemplated the possibility that my own mother would be Lee's enabler.

<hr />

Time and time again, victims of trauma are told to "move on" and "get over it" after their abuser has left the picture. People who offer this "solution" simply have no understanding of the nature of trauma. Removing the perpetrator of trauma doesn't fix the pain an abuser caused, just as removing someone from a fire doesn't heal the pain of their burns. The residual, spiritual pain of trauma long outlasts the physical presence of the one who inflicted it, and what those well-meaning officers failed to realize is that Lee didn't hurt only my body, he broke my spirit. While you can place a

> You can't repair *spiritual* brokenness with physical tools.

bandage on a cut or use a splint to set a broken bone, you can't repair *spiritual* brokenness with physical tools. Yes, I survived in the sense that I was physically intact, but the post-traumatic pain I was forced to wade through served as a constant reminder of the trauma itself.

Mom didn't say anything about what had happened to me until a few days after we left the police station.

"It happens," she said with a shrug.

Her no-big-deal attitude, while possibly intended to help me, simply made me feel more ashamed. The woman who I had thought was my personal superhero had now reduced the most traumatic experience of my young life down to a casual stroll through the park. I felt exposed, unprotected, unworthy. And as the days went by, the emotional shame of the experience hurt worse than the physical pain. In my shame I felt that I was a mistake. I felt that I had not only done something to deserve what happened to me, but I felt that my very existence was the reason it happened.

Having Lee arrested didn't heal me. His absence didn't remove the presence of shame. Maybe you have been there.

Maybe you're there now. The pain of your past continues to stir shame in your present. You may have even felt guilty about what happened, but at some point that guilt became deeper, darker, and more ingrained in your identity. That guilt became like a mile-marker in your life. It is something you want to escape from, but every time you think you've made it beyond the pain, you look behind you to check your distance from the mile-marker that created the guilt and are reminded of how inescapable the past is. But I want you to know that, when God heals us, he removes the mile-markers of past pain.

> When God heals us, he removes the mile-markers of past pain.

When guilt begins to define who we are, it is no longer guilt at all. It's shame. We feel guilty about something we *did* and its impact on the people we care about. We can feel guilty about things we didn't even do, simply because of its impact on the people we care about. Shame, on the other hand, is entirely different. Shame doesn't only cause us to feel guilty about *what* happened, it also assumes the responsibility for what happened and attributes it to our *identity*. Brené Brown defines this by saying, "Guilt says I *made* a mistake; shame says I *am* a mistake."[1] There are things in our past that we aren't proud of, but if we allow those things to define who we are, we will live in a state of shame. As I matured in my walk with God, I realized that the things Lee did to me and the things Mom said to me had created a broken identity in which I saw myself as worthless. It was only when I saw myself through the filter of God's Word that I realized I was made for so much more than just surviving. I was made to thrive and flourish. And you were too.

When I was a girl, surviving meant trying to be invisible

at home. I didn't speak unless spoken to. I stayed in my room unless called to another room. I immersed myself in books at a young age because in them I found an escape hatch to safe alternative realities. I didn't see people as safe, so to keep people away, I kept to myself at home, and I acted out at school to isolate myself. And it worked. I had unresolved hurts that no one cared to excavate, so I dealt with them by imploding at home and exploding at school.

Maybe surviving looks similar for you. We all have our strategies. Maybe to the outside world you're the life of the party, but to the people who know you best you're angry, difficult, or reserved. The energy you exert to make others like the person you're pretending to be doesn't leave any energy to *actually* be nice at home. Perhaps it's reversed and you're a loner in the outside world and clingy with the people who know you best. You keep coworkers at bay but won't let your spouse or children out of your sight for fear of what might happen to them because of what happened to you. You're a different person in different situations because you aren't sure when you can let your guard down. But even when uncertainty is the only thing you're certain of, there is hope and an opportunity to thrive through God.

> Even when uncertainty is the only thing you're certain of, there is hope and an opportunity to thrive through God.

Uncertainty can breed fear, and fear can change the way we show up in the world. But the Bible lets us know that God hasn't given us a spirit of fear but instead gives us power, love, and a sound mind (2 Timothy 1:7 NKJV). In God we have hope no matter how difficult our path to healing is.

Vernita was just eighteen when she gave birth to a baby girl in rural, segregated Mississippi, and she moved away shortly afterward. The little girl spent the first six years of her life in the care of her grandmother. She was brilliant and even learned to read before the age of three, but she was regularly punished for anything her grandmother didn't like. One time, when the young girl went to the well to get some water, she became intrigued by the water and played in it with her fingers. Her grandmother saw it and beat her so badly that the girl bled from the welts on her back. When she put on her dress for church, the welts bled through the dress, and her grandmother beat her again for getting blood on the dress.

At age six the girl left her grandmother to move to Milwaukee with her mother, but while there, the woman in charge of the house her mother lived in made the girl sleep on the porch. At nine years old, she was raped. The man who raped her took her to get ice cream, with blood still streaming down her leg. She continued to be abused and molested between the ages of ten and fourteen, when she found out she was pregnant. Two weeks after she gave birth, the baby died. In that baby's life she had built hope for a new life of her own, and when it died, her hope for the future died too. But that summer, she took an acting class for the first time, and she allowed the pain, turmoil, and emotion of her life to emerge on stage. She felt a cathartic purge as the thoughts and feelings she had kept trapped inside were finally forced to the outside.

Although her healing did not happen immediately, she discovered over many years that giving voice to her pain was the first step toward healing from it. And her voice has become a source of healing, hope, and inspiration for millions. The baby girl who was originally named Orpah, but was called Oprah because of mispronunciation, has become one of the most recognized names in the world. And yet behind the celebrity, wealth, power, and influence is a woman who had to discover the power to rise from her past. A woman like you. A woman like me. In discovering her voice and shining a light on her shame, she was able to redefine her future and chart a path toward success on her own terms.

God hasn't made us to *merely* survive. He has made us to shine.

He sees you and your struggles and wants us all to know that our past is simply the prologue to our destiny. You may be at the beginning of your journey to healing, and you may not even believe it's possible to heal from what hurts you so deeply. I ask you to trust me for just a little while longer so you can discover what God wants you to know: you were formed in your mother's womb with a purpose and destiny that only *you* can fulfill. You are the only you that ever was and ever will be. The reason your fingerprints are unique to you is because your fingerprints are the "passcode" that unlocks the uniquely crafted, individually mandated calling on your life. How unfortunate it is, then, that so many of us live our lives as photocopies of another person when God has made us an original. I see you. God sees you. And this world needs all of you—healthy and whole.

> You are the only you that ever was and ever will be.

So now, let's do the hard work together.

Chapter 2

The Enemy Within

"What I do with my money is *my* bidness, Mary! Who you think you are sassin' me 'bout *my* money?"

"Sunny, I ain't sassin'! These children need to eat! You know how much they pay me to clean those houses. I don't make enough money to feed twelve kids by myself. I—"

"See, dat's your problem right there! Ain't nobody make you have twelve kids! Dat's *yo* fault! I pays fa dis house so y'all can have a roof over ya heads! What I do with the rest of *my* money is up to me. I'll be back when I gets back."

As he made his way through the tiny living room crowded with children of all ages, he stopped to pat my young mother, one of his favorites, on the head. She beamed with pride at the gesture as he made his way out the front door. He never glanced back at my grandmother, but if he had, he would have seen the once-vibrant woman he had swept off her feet with promises of a good life, wiping tears onto the apron of her maid's uniform. Her eyes were tired, swollen, and blackened by the fists he regularly pounded into her head for any reason. Or no reason at all.

After years of him blowing his money by gambling and drinking after a day of collecting garbage, she knew what to expect when he returned home broke and drunk later that night. But she straightened her back, cleared her throat, and directed the army of little people living in their two-bedroom house.

"Patricia, straighten up this living room."

"Kelly, get those dishes clean for dinner."

"Barbara, warm that pot of beans, and start a pot of rice."

"Dana, make sure the babies get baths."

"Everybody else, get yourself cleaned up for dinner."

". . . and, Frances . . . stay in this house."

———— ∞∞∞ ————

My mom started running away from home at a young age. The ninth of twelve children, she was five the first time her mother noticed she was missing. No one knew or asked why she left. Maybe it was the sound of her mother's screams at the hands of her father. Maybe it was the discomfort of six people having to sleep head to toe in a bed made for two. Maybe she was hungry from eating grease sandwiches in the absence of real food. Maybe it was all of this and more. Mom first slipped away for a few hours to play with a neighbor, then a few hours became a full day, and a full day became a few days. Her family rarely knew where she went or what she was doing. But she would often come home to find that her parents hadn't even realized she was gone.

When she *was* home, her siblings often wished she wasn't. Mom had an anger streak that lacked boundaries or reason. In the third grade, she got expelled from school after pushing a teacher down a flight of stairs for telling her to get in line. Another time she pulled a knife on her older sister and lunged at her with every intention of stabbing her. When her father found out about it, instead of punishing my mom, he punished her sister for "starting it." Mom looked on, smiling smugly, while her sister got a beating. Rules didn't apply to my mom. Maybe my grandmother was so exhausted by the time my mom was born that she gave up, or maybe my grandfather let her violence slide because he saw his own tendencies in her behavior. For Mom, dysfunction was normal.

In her teen years, she was labeled as "wild." She did what she wanted when she wanted and dared anyone, including her mother, to question her. But her behavior belied her beauty. She was gorgeous. Boys liked her at an early age. So did grown men. When my father caught sight of her at a house party, he noticed her "high yellow" complexion and determined to ask for her number. But being a dark-skinned man, he wasn't sure whether she would pay him any attention, so he did the only thing he knew to do. When the next record came on blaring James Brown's "I Feel Good," he strolled calmly to the center of the dancing crowd, just within eyeshot of my mom, and let it rip.

To everyone's shock and delight, my dad danced *exactly* like James Brown—footwork, splits, and all. He was suddenly the coolest cat at the party, and while multiple women tried to get his attention, he walked straight up to my mom and said, "Hey, pretty lady. My name is D'Wayne. Mind if I call you some time?" Since Mom didn't have a phone at home, she said, "You can't call me, but we can go get a soda together," and they made plans to go on a date a couple of days later.

Not long after their first date, Dad knew he wanted to marry my mom. That's when he found out that his new love was fifteen. He was twenty-one. He was shocked because she looked and acted much older, so he decided not to let her age faze him. He asked my grandpa for her hand in marriage, and given the chance to have one less mouth to feed, Grandpa said yes. They wed in the summer of 1967, and it didn't take long for Dad to find out he got more than he bargained for. After the "fairy dust" of the wedding faded and they settled into married life, they began to have minor disagreements, as all newly married couples do. While my father would simply shrug a disagreement off, Mom would become consumed with rage. Their first argument ended with her throwing everything within arm's reach at him.

Despite the emotional roller coaster, Dad wanted to start having children right away. He was raised in a home environment very different from Mom's, with two parents who never argued in front of their children. His father was a devout Christian and worked hard to instill character in his children's lives. Dad idolized his father, so now that he was married, he wanted to start building his own family. But Mom wasn't interested in settling down and raising children. She liked to party and didn't want rules or responsibilities to infringe on her freedom. This included any "rules" about being a wife.

When Mom got angry with Dad, she would disappear for days, just as she had done as a child. When she decided to return home, she would offer no apology or explanation for leaving. She left so frequently that Dad didn't know whether she would be home after work, even if they hadn't had a fight. He also suspected she wasn't alone when she left. Dad was a sharp dresser, funny, and friendly, but he also battled his own insecurities. He was born with a leg deformity. One leg was slightly shorter than the other, causing him to limp when he walked. Kids made fun of him relentlessly.

Between that and being called "darkie" his entire life, he treated my mom as if she were a prize he shouldn't have won. And perhaps because of this, he turned a blind eye to problems even Stevie Wonder could see.

Trauma changes you. It changes the way you show up in the world and changes what you accept. Both my mom and my dad brought trauma into their marriage, and since they didn't know what to call it or how to fix it, they simply entered a pattern of argue, disappear, reappear, argue, disappear, reappear. How many of us do the same thing? Even when we know something is wrong, instead of working to fix it or even just trying to *name* it, we either run away or pretend everything's okay while the house burns to the ground around us.

But what we don't fix in ourselves simply gets swept under the rug of our children, causing generational trauma. The violent way my grandfather treated my grandmother later manifested in the violent way my mother treated my father. And while my father may have thought he was being loving by not challenging Mom's behavior, he was actually

> What we don't fix in ourselves simply gets swept under the rug of our children, causing generational trauma.

enabling her self-destruction and his emotional degradation. When God made Adam and Eve, he told them to "subdue" the earth (Genesis 1:28). We weren't made to be doormats; we were made to *lead*. But when our spirits are broken, we take one of two paths: we run or we succumb.

Running is what we do when we physically remove

ourselves from whatever triggers our unresolved pain. Maybe we hang up on people when we get angry, or maybe we leave the house in a fit of rage after an argument with our spouse. Either way, we are leaving the situation instead of addressing the root of what triggered our anger in the first place. This was my mom's method.

> When our spirits are broken, we take one of two paths: we run or we succumb.

My dad, on the other hand, would succumb. This happens when we shut down when confronted with something that triggers our unresolved pain. Maybe we tune out the person trying to tell us we hurt them, or maybe we simply nod and say, "I'm sorry," to try to move on from the issue. Neither running nor succumbing fixes the brokenness that leads to taking those actions; they simply become entrenched in our identity. And this is why the path toward healing must begin with self-awareness.

———— ∞∞∞ ————

"Congratulations, again, ma'am. Our entire team is so happy for—" Click. Dial tone.

"Wayne! Wayne!" Mom yelled for my dad at the top of her lungs.

"Yes? What's wrong?"

"I hope you're happy now! I can't believe I let you do this to me."

"What's the problem? What did I do?"

"That was the doctor's office. I'm pregnant."

The day Mom got the call that she was pregnant, Dad couldn't contain himself. They had been married for thirteen years by then, and he desperately wanted to be a father.

Mom, on the other hand, didn't want children, and she cried at the news. She was angry. The thought of having a child made her feel trapped. She had promised herself she would never be like her mom—stuck in a house full of children, working two or three jobs to feed them. She had even avoided babysitting her nieces and nephews because she didn't want to be tied down with a child.

But my dad couldn't have been more excited. He called all his family and friends to share the good news. He even went to the corner store and bought cigars in anticipation of the day to come. But what happened next was not part of his plan.

Six months into the pregnancy, Dad developed severe stomach pain and began vomiting blood. He went to the local clinic to run tests, and when the results came back, the doctor asked him to come in for a meeting.

"Mr. Collins, the news isn't good. I've looked at your X-rays, and I see what appear to be large tumors in your stomach. I'll need to do a biopsy to confirm, but what I see looks like cancer."

"I don't understand. Cancer? Isn't that an old person's disease? I'm thirty-four. That can't be right."

"Cancer isn't based on age, sir. I'm really sorry to give you this news."

"Well, what else could it be? Maybe my stomach is just swollen. Is there something else it could be?"

"From what I see, I'm afraid not. I want to do a biopsy just to be sure, though."

"If it is . . . if it is . . . cancer . . . what would my options be?"

"Let's talk about that once I confirm what we're dealing with, okay? Just lie back. This is going to be a bit uncomfortable, but I need you to be still. I have to put this tube down your throat to get to your stomach."

As Dad made his way home that night, he didn't want to believe what he knew to be true. He could hardly see the cars in front of him through his tear-blurred eyes. How could he have waited thirteen years to be a father, only to never meet his daughter? His heart broke at the thought of never seeing me. Never holding me. Never sitting in the auditorium to watch me graduate from high school. Never locking arms with me as I nervously look up at him before he walks me down the aisle.

The next day he got the call that confirmed the doctor's suspicion. And it was even worse. The cancer was advanced and aggressive.

"How long do I have, doc? I have a baby girl on the way."

"I . . . I would say six months at the most. I'm terribly sorry, sir. I really, really am."

Dad hung up the phone and broke down. When he gathered himself, he determined to fight back as hard as he could. For me. He had kept his health issues private up until that moment. He hadn't even told Mom. Once he did tell her, she couldn't believe it. He slowly began to tell family and friends his diagnosis, adding, "But I ain't going nowhere before I hold my baby girl."

He expressed to several people that his greatest fear was that I wouldn't remember him, so when I was born, he gathered all the energy he had and began an Olympic sprint of memory-making. He loved baseball and bought me a personalized, child-sized baseball bat with the intention of teaching me how to play the game. In an effort to savor every second, he hardly let anyone else hold me, change me, feed me, or take me out of his sight. He hoped this might permanently imprint the look of his face and the feel of his embrace in my mind.

Despite being given six months to live, Dad was there on my first birthday, dressed up in a clown suit to make me laugh. His normally athletic frame is visibly gaunt in the photos, and his usually deep ebony complexion was noticeably pale and ashen. But he did everything possible to make me smile that day. And it was the first and last birthday he was able to spend with me.

Every parent imagines that their children will outlive them, but no parent imagines that their children won't remember them. My dad waited thirteen years of marriage to become a father. He endured Mom's constant anger and abandonment because he believed the fruit of his patience would eventually yield children. I imagine he must have been angry to know Mom denied him the gift of fatherhood for so many years, only to have death deny it again once he had finally attained it.

The pain my dad had to contend with is unimaginable, yet many of us have contended with similar pain, the pain of broken expectations. You expected one thing to happen, only to have the complete opposite happen. And it hurts. You expected your spouse to be faithful, only to learn they had an affair. You expected your child would be safe in the care of a loved one, only to learn they violated your child's innocence. You expected a friend to repay the money you loaned them sacrificially, but instead of repaying you, they've been sharing their latest vacation pictures on Instagram. When we don't have the tools to excavate *and* extricate the pain of broken expectations, the residual hurt seeps into and infects our relationships. This is why the most difficult work we have to do is in ourselves, not in others.

My grandparents and parents are case studies in this truth. Before dysfunction ever showed up at my doorstep, broken expectations took up residence in each of their lives. My mom's father had determined to get more out of life than his sharecropping parents, who were just one generation out of slavery. His move up north to New Jersey was his way of putting that dream into practice. He envisioned landing a well-paying factory job and promised my grandmother a nice home, exotic trips, and a lifetime of romance. But his reality in an America where black people were legally barred from well-paying jobs consisted of being denied every job he applied for, except the one job he didn't want—garbage collector. He collected garbage in the sweltering heat of summer and the bitter cold of New Jersey winter, while his white boss called him "boy" and often didn't pay him his full week's wages. He lost his legs later in life from the damage caused by walking miles in waist-high snow for hours at a time.

> The most difficult work we have to do is in ourselves.

Grandpa returned home smelling like garbage every day, and despite the love that twinkled in Grandma's eyes, all he could see when he looked in them was the reflection of disdain and shame he felt for himself. The first time he hit her, he was immediately sorry and shocked, but as his self-loathing became more entrenched, he transferred his anger to her with daily pushes, slaps, and punches. Grandma grew up in the generation that didn't "air dirty laundry," so she tried to hide her bruises beneath layers of makeup, making her look years older than her actual age. He continued to beat her when the children came along, creating an atmosphere of fear and helplessness that chiseled my mother's temperament from birth. Although my mom was labeled "wild" for her defiant behavior, I've wondered whether her behavior was just a cry for help, as mine was.

My father had been ridiculed for his dark skin his entire life, so he often dressed in layers of clothing before going outside in an effort not to get darker from the sun. When he met my mom, he was already nursing his own identity crisis.

Each of us is part of a generational tapestry of pain and dysfunction, and we must confront what lies within us before we can address what's happening around us. For some of us, the dysfunction was overt and left the type of physical, emotional, and psychological scars that everyone around us can see. But for others of us, the dysfunction was subtle. Alcoholism, addiction, neglect, poverty, and criticism are things that can damage our spirit. These can manifest themselves in a multitude of ways, such as a lack of trust in others, no matter how trustworthy they prove themselves to be, or a need to buy only name brand clothes and shoes to combat internal feelings of being "less than." Dysfunction has touched each of us, which means we all have an opportunity to experience the healing power of God's grace.

> Each of us is part of a generational tapestry of pain and dysfunction, and we must confront what lies within us before we can address what's happening around us.

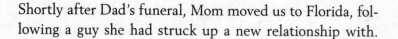

Shortly after Dad's funeral, Mom moved us to Florida, following a guy she had struck up a new relationship with.

That relationship ended shortly after we arrived there, and a string of boyfriends paraded in and out of our lives over the course of two years. Then Lee moved in with us. I was four years old and clearly remember the day I met him. He was white, and I remember being excited to show him to my friends when he picked me up from school so I could say I was half white. Lee was more like a kid than an adult to me. He would get on the floor and play whatever make-believe scenario I was acting out with my Barbie and Ken dolls. As an only child, I had a busy imagination, and Lee was always willing to enter my imaginary world. I started calling him Dad because I desperately wanted a father. What I didn't understand was that Lee's befriending me was simply him grooming me for what he really wanted.

Our past is not a linear chronology of events. Our past is an intricate web of experiences, relationships, beliefs, and reactions we live through, both firsthand and vicariously through the experiences, relationships, beliefs, and reactions of the people who shape us. The journey to rise from my past required gaining an understanding of how generational layers of dysfunction shaped me. The complex interconnections among the stories of my grandpa, grandma, mother, and father have proven foundational to the narrative of my own life because why I do things can always be traced back to who taught me to do them.

> Our past is not a linear chronology of events.

In what ways have the people in your life shaped you? When you face a challenge, what similarities do you see between how you behave and how those who raised you behave? I see my mom in me during times of distress, because when I'm hurt, I run away. I'll hang up in the middle of a heated conversation, leave the room in the middle of an argument, or simply block a person's number when I no longer wish to engage with them. My first inclination is to run when I'm hurt, rather than addressing what's hurting me and seeking a solution, and the root of that response is a fear of rejection. I often believe that the other person is going to abandon me at some point, so I do it for them instead of waiting for the inevitable. It's a defense mechanism that allows me to maintain some type of control over the situation, even though it still ultimately hurts.

Maybe you grew up with a father whom you could never please. No matter how many awards you won, he was always disappointed that you didn't do more. Maybe your mother constantly criticized your appearance. You would put on your nicest outfit and work hard to look your best, but she always managed to point out the tiniest imperfection. Maybe it was a teacher who never called on you when you raised your hand, causing you to doubt whether what you had to say mattered at all. These experiences become woven together into our identity over time.

When I was eleven, I broke my toe on a chair leg while chasing a friend around a room. The pain was unbearable, and when we arrived at the doctor's office, the first thing they did was touch my toe. Big mistake. I screamed like a banshee from the pain and told them never to touch that toe again. The problem was that repairing the broken bone required them to touch it, causing tremendous pain. Have you found yourself similarly refusing to allow anyone to touch your wound? When they get too close and manage to push on your wound, you yell, scream, isolate yourself, or cut them off, whatever you have to do to keep people out of your broken places.

A great leadership assessment I've taken and used with my teams in business is called a 360 review, which gathers candid feedback from an employee's manager (above), peers (across), and reports (below) to provide an accurate assessment of how the employee is perceived. It's effective at uncovering blind spots because while you might be able to dismiss or explain away *one* person's feedback, it's difficult to do that when everyone in your professional circle says the same thing. An area I have consistently scored low in is "receptivity to feedback." In other words, I have a difficult time with criticism. And it's absolutely true. Similar to not wanting that doctor to touch my broken toe because it hurt, I don't take criticism well, personally or professionally, because it touches my deepest pain, the pain that I'm unworthy.

I grew up being physically punished for the slightest infraction, so I developed a perfectionist mentality in an effort to avoid Mom's anger. I tried to anticipate what she wanted me to do, and I would do it "perfectly" to make her happy. But when I carried this approach into my professional career, I didn't anticipate that "perfection" is in the eye of the beholder. When I was appointed to my first executive role at age twenty-three, I spent *hours upon hours* preparing reports with the hope of achieving perfection, only to present them in a meeting and have people ask questions I had never considered. Colleagues also routinely overlooked my extra effort to make the presentation look "pretty," instead focusing on the facts and figures. I left meetings devastated from benign questions and felt personally attacked when someone didn't agree with a recommendation I made. My position on the organizational chart said I was "successful," but I felt defeated and undervalued.

Our past pain manifests in our present, and this is why self-awareness is key to defeating the enemy within ourselves. Self-reflection is critical to progress.

Perhaps you're fighting with a spouse over how much money they've spent, or maybe you're irritated with a coworker who never follows through on projects, leaving you to complete the work. The question you need ask is: Why does this bother me? When it comes to your spouse, are you truly low on money, or does seeing a certain number in your bank account give you the type of security you should have only in God? Why do you keep picking up your coworker's slack? Is *your* job truly at risk if they don't complete their work, or does having them lean on you in a crunch make you feel as though you matter and you need their validation?

The brokenness in us can lead us to take *personally* what we should take *seriously*. The distinction is that when we take something personally, we make the issue about our identity. In the case of the spouse who overspends, if our anger is coming from the fear of financial problems making us "look bad" to people, we have taken their behavior personally.

> The hurt *within* us is the filter for everything *around* us.

If, instead, our anger is rooted in the concern for our family's future, we have taken their habits seriously. The difference is found in asking the question: Do I feel this way because of what this *says* about me, or do I feel this way because of what this is doing to the people I care about?

Past hurt can cause us to see life through a lens that

views everyone and everything as out to hurt us, not because they truly are but because the hurt *within* us is the filter for everything *around* us. Just as my grandfather saw my grandmother as the enemy, despite her only wanting the best for him and their family, the hurt we use to filter the people and situations in our lives will make our friends our foes. When anger, insecurity, jealousy, and revenge well up inside us, we have to acknowledge their presence and evict them through prayer. The past pain we don't evict will eventually evict our future purpose.

The popular television host was very successful according to the trappings of success that defined his life. His highly rated shows took him around the world to enjoy the best food and experiences life had to offer. Yet on June 8, 2018, Anthony Bourdain hung himself in his extravagant room at Le Chambard hotel in Kaysersberg, France. He was in France filming a new season of his popular show *Parts Unknown*, a trip that included exquisite food, expensive wine, and laughter with his crew. No one suspected what was in his mind. Maybe he didn't either.

Bourdain's suicide was called an "impulsive act" preceded by "troubling signs." His toxicology tests were negative for narcotics, and his colleagues who traveled with him were mystified when they learned what had happened. How does someone who has everything decide that their life is no longer worth living? We will never know what was in his mind, but if a man who seemed to have everything can feel he has nothing worth living for, we are *all* vulnerable to the impact of unaddressed trauma.

Maybe you have been using the deception of deflection. You tell jokes or blow up at people in hopes of creating enough buffer to keep people from getting too close and touching your wounds. But our journey toward self-discovery will begin when we decide to work on what's broken inside us instead of using deflection as a defense mechanism to keep people away from our pain. Doing this will require us to take an inventory of ourselves—the fears, hurts, bitterness, and unforgiveness we're incubating in our hearts. When we become self-aware, we can finally put a name to the enemy we're fighting.

> When we become self-aware, we can finally put a name to the enemy we're fighting.

Start by grabbing a notepad and recounting the scenarios in which you behaved with loved ones in ways you regret. Maybe you lost your temper with your child, or maybe you've been taking solace in conversations with an old love that would destroy your spouse if they found out. Once you have an example, it's time to get honest and ask yourself the tough questions. What was the story in your mind that made you take that course of action? What were you afraid of? What part of your identity felt under attack? What was at stake that you had to protect and fight for? Now let's go a level deeper. *Who* taught you to fear that thing? *Who* challenged your identity that way before? *Who* made you think the thing you were fighting to protect was vulnerable?

When you've gone through this exercise, it is time for us to explore the next most important question: *Why?*

Chapter 3

Releasing the Why

"Nona, I need to talk to you for a minute. Let's go out on the back patio," Mom said as she stood in the doorway of my bedroom.

"Did I do something wrong?" My seven-year-old mind thought through everything I did that morning. Did I leave the box of cereal on the counter? Did I forget my dolls on the living room floor?

"No. No, I just want us to get some fresh air and talk about something."

I closed the book I was reading and left it on my bed to follow her outside. I noticed the patches of gold-tipped grass springing up in the backyard. The air was cool and crisp against my face as the season transitioned from winter to spring.

"Nona, I need to ask you something. Come, sit down."

"Okay."

"What would you think about Lee coming back to live with us?"

My heart quickened. "I . . . I . . . I don't want him to come back," I said, lowering my eyes to the ground, having sensed that the question was rhetorical.

"Well . . . look," she said as she stood up and glared down at me. "He's been away for a while now, and I need help with these bills. I can't afford all this stuff you want, anyway." Then she added with an air of authority and entitlement, "Besides, this is my house, and I make the decisions, so he's coming back."

With a sense of finality hanging in the air like a blade poised to strike, she turned away from me and walked into the house without looking back. The sound of the sliding glass door slamming closed made me jump, piercing my heart with its sharpness. She left me alone in the cold and my seven-year-old mind tried to process what was about to happen. But I couldn't.

Mom took me with her to pick Lee up from jail on the day of his release. This man, who was legally prohibited from coming within one thousand feet of any place frequented by children for the rest of his life, was now being welcomed back into the home of the child he had violated. When he got into the car that day, his face was smug. If he had any doubt before, he now knew with complete assurance that Mom needed him more than he needed her. Her taking him back was a permanent "get out of jail free" card that licensed him to do whatever he wanted. I felt completely defeated that day, and although I was young, I knew that nothing I said in the future would matter. I retreated deep within myself and taught myself not to feel. How not to exist. How not to care what happened to me. He abused me repeatedly over the next four years, so I learned to pretend I wasn't there when it happened. I was air. Anywhere else but where I was.

Life didn't make sense to me, so I accepted the "problem child" label at school and decided to live down to my teacher's expectations. My second-grade teacher routinely made an example of me in front of my classmates, calling me disruptive and telling me to stop bothering other kids who "have a future." I didn't do my classwork or homework, but since I still passed her exams, she assumed I was cheating off students sitting near me. She punished me by moving my desk to the farthest corner of the classroom, away from everyone. Although she meant to ostracize me, I loved being in that corner by myself. I could draw without being bothered, and she never called on me to answer questions. And to her surprise, I still passed the exams.

All her progress reports said the same thing: "Nona is smart but disruptive." I got all Es (exceptional) and Ss (satisfactory) in the academic subjects, but never got above an N (insufficient) for conduct. My mom never went back to school after being expelled in the third grade, so she took vicarious pride in my grades, thinking they were a reflection of her own parenting prowess and telling her siblings and friends what I got on my report cards. It always struck me how she could call me such hurtful names in one moment, then brag about my grades the next. I used to love overhearing those phone calls about my grades because it was the one time I felt as though she might have been proud of me. But I knew in my heart that the calls were more about her than me. Being able to take credit for my grades made her feel good about herself, but she never considered that my grades weren't *because of* her. They were *in spite of* her.

Shortly after Lee moved back home, Mom started throwing parties at our house most weekends. She would openly drink and smoke weed in front of me, and there were always strangers in our house. I showed up to school many Monday mornings sleepy because the sound of reggae music blasting and people laughing all night long made it difficult to sleep. One time when I was eight, Lee gave me a beer during a party, and since it looked like a soda can, I took a sip, then immediately spit it out. It tasted like cold liquid garbage to me, and watching people drink from those cans over and over again left me perplexed. When he saw my reaction, he went and grabbed me a wine cooler instead. I took a sip and it tasted like juice, but there was a bitterness in it that made me stop. Mom blew smoke in my face several times as a joke, and it made me cough and made my eyes burn. I decided against smoking and drinking at that young age.

With the constant partying, the reason I didn't do my homework was because there wasn't a quiet place to concentrate. When it *was* quiet, I just wanted to sleep. I became chronically exhausted and got to a place mentally where I didn't think there was much to look forward to each day, so food became my comfort. Mom always had a refrigerator and pantry full of food, so I ate anything that wasn't nailed down to medicate my pain. By the time I entered third grade, I was at least twice as heavy as my classmates, and I got teased relentlessly. When I got home, Mom would pick up where the kids left off, saying, "You're big as a house, Nona." In addition to comments about my weight, I remember several times when she was high that she called me a "little whore." I didn't know what that meant, but the way she said it communicated a vileness that didn't require definition.

When I was in the fourth grade, to the teachers and administrators at school, I was just another defiant kid who needed an attitude adjustment. But on the inside I was dying. Mom and Lee were fighting in the living room one weekend afternoon when she asked me a question that I answered truthfully without the context of their argument. Apparently my answer was the same as Lee's, making her wrong in whatever they were arguing about. With a look of wild rage in her eyes, she lunged at me and grabbed me around the neck, then threw me on the couch and started choking me. I can't remember whether she stopped choking me on her own or whether Lee stopped her, but I ran from the living room into my bedroom and locked the door, then hid inside my closet and closed the doors. Tears streamed down my face, and pain burned in my throat. I was still gasping for air as I sat in that dark closet. I cried myself to sleep while sitting on top of a pile of dirty clothes and shoes.

When I woke up and opened my closet doors, the house was silent and it was no longer light outside. I cautiously opened my bedroom door and listened but didn't hear anyone. I slipped out of my room into the dark house and silently walked out the side door to see whether Mom's car was gone. It was. I walked back inside the house and looked around to see whether Lee was there, but he was gone too. I was home alone, so I made my way to where Mom kept the laundry supplies. I had recently watched a talk show that featured parents whose children had died from unforeseen dangers inside their homes—from a television that toppled off an unstable dresser and crushed a child to death to a container of bleach that poisoned and killed a toddler who drank it after opening an unsecured cap. I remembered the bleach story and tried to find the bottle Mom usually kept in the house, but the only thing in the supply closet was laundry detergent. So I poured a capful and forced it down, then went to my bedroom and lay down on the floor to die. When you're dying on the inside, physical death doesn't seem like such a bad alternative.

Instead of dying, I ended up throwing up all night. At one point after Mom came home, she heard me throwing up and yelled from another room, "Serves you right, always eating up all my food!" She never came to check on me, making my feeling of inadequacy run even deeper.

When I finally stopped throwing up and realized my plan didn't work, I was sad. But more than sad, I was angry and confused. I hadn't asked Mom to have me, so why didn't she love me? What had I done that was so bad that she didn't care whether I was dead or alive? Would it be better if I ran away from home? Would it be better if she *did* get rid of me and I went to live with strangers? What could possibly be worse? Why was this happening to me?

⸛

How many times have you found yourself trying to make sense of what is truly senseless? While I believe that the facts of our past matter, I've discovered in my journey to freedom that the *meaning* we give to the facts of our past matter more than the facts themselves. What happened to me was painful, and the memory of the facts still hurts to this day, yet the pain I experience today isn't about the facts of what happened; the pain is because of what those facts have come to mean *about myself.*

> The *meaning* we give to the facts of our past matter more than the facts themselves.

Mattering to people is a deep need of mine, probably more than most people because so many years of my life were spent being treated like I wasn't wanted until I could be used. To this day, it means so much to me when a friend recognizes my birthday or reaches out to check on me for no reason at all. And it's equally painful for me when I realize a person contacts me only when they want something from me, when they determine that my only value to them is to the extent that I give them something they want for themselves.

Maybe Mom allowed Lee to hurt me because his disability check was more valuable to her than I was. Why wasn't I worth more to her? Maybe Lee hurt me because he saw something in me that made him think I wanted it. Why did I make him think I wanted it? Maybe Mom was right when she said he wouldn't have done what he did if I had just kept my legs closed. Why didn't I fight harder or do more to protect myself? Maybe I brought everything on myself because I am fundamentally defective. Why am I so worthless?

The more I allowed myself to be consumed with this thought pattern, the more I claimed ownership of what happened to me, and the more ownership I took, the more shame I felt. I've come to term this cycle the "hopelessness hole" because the further you dig into it, the further there is to dig. There are no answers to the questions no matter how many you ask. Maybe . . . why . . . maybe . . . why . . . maybe . . . why. And since I couldn't make sense of my pain in a way that made it go away, I instead created my own form of truth to explain the unexplainable. A truth that always placed me as the one responsible for the "why."

Have you been there? A place where the only explanations you can come up with are the ones that simply beg more questions? A place where the only explanation that makes sense to you is that the reason it happened was because "something was wrong with *me*"? When we ask questions that have no explanation that can ease our pain, we inevitably turn inward and charge ourselves with responsibility for the hurt we feel. This is why I need you to know you are not what happened to you.

When we internalize external dysfunction, we often tend to believe *we* are defective. The day my fifth-grade teacher

You are not what happened to you.

pulled me out of line on the way to art class and told me I would never be anything more than a failure, I didn't cry as she pointed her finger in my face and said those words. But inside, my heart broke. When I made it home that afternoon and found the house empty, I grabbed a butcher knife and went into my bathroom to slit my wrists. I had heard a story about someone killing themselves that way, so I cut my wrists deep enough for blood to flow down my hands into the sink but missed my ulnar artery. I became lightheaded while I stood over the sink, but the cuts clotted and dried while I waited. After a while, I grabbed a washcloth from under the sink, wet it with warm water, and wiped the blood away. I then put two bandages on the cuts and went to my room to lie down. My second suicide attempt didn't work, but the permanent scar inside my left wrist is a daily reminder of how God's grace works, even when we don't want it to.

I was disappointed again, but something in me realized that my continuing to live wasn't by accident. I didn't know anything about God at that time, but there was a sense in my heart that death wasn't the answer. Having now been given the gift of hindsight and a relationship with Jesus, it's so evident that the hand of God was on my life from a young age. I thought I was alone and battling my pain by myself, but the truth is, God was right there with me. Loving me.

Protecting me from my despair. Protecting me from myself. People who survive trauma know that you never "get over" what happened. For some, they teach themselves to live with a pain that dulls over time but never disappears. But given how much God loves us, I believe he wants more for us than to simply live with dulled pain. I believe he wants to mend the cracks and crevices in our hearts *completely*.

This truth is shown beautifully in the story of Lazarus. In John 11 we find the well-known story of Jesus raising Lazarus from the dead. On a scale from one to five, where one is "freshly" dead and five is "very" dead, Lazarus was a five. He had been buried in his tomb for four days when Jesus arrived in town, so the funeral was over, and his sisters' grieving process was in full swing. But something important happens in this story that goes beyond raising Lazarus from the dead.

In John 11:43–44 we find the following words: "When he had said this, Jesus called in a loud voice, 'Lazarus, come out!' The dead man came out, his hands and feet wrapped with strips of linen, and a cloth around his face." Lazarus walked out of the tomb alive but still bound in his grave clothes. His grave clothes made him a "dead man walking." Jesus didn't just say, "All right, everyone. Mission accomplished," and leave Lazarus to walk around Bethany like a mummy. No. Verse 44 continues with Jesus saying, "Take off the grave clothes and let him go." I believe that Jesus is calling each of us to rise from the tomb of past pain. And Jesus wants to release us, as he did with Lazarus, from everything that signals what happened to us—the grave clothes of painful memories, broken identities, fractured hearts, and the notion that we're defective.

Grave clothes are for those who have died, not for the

living. Jesus wanted to release Lazarus from his grave clothes because the tomb was not where he belonged, just as Jesus wants to release us from the trappings of our past, where we have never belonged.

"Why did this happen to me?" is a question that holds us back and links us to a past where we no longer belong. But Jesus's invitation to all of us is to step forward, free of the past, and into a future where we can walk securely with him.

On the evening of September 24, 1942, Dr. Viktor Frankl kissed his wife on the forehead as they both prepared to go to bed. It was a tender, familiar gesture—one they repeated hundreds of times during their marriage. As many of us do, he drifted to sleep while running through his mental to-do list for the next day. Little did he know that his life would be irreversibly changed within a few short hours. In the wee hours of September 25, 1942, the Nazi army rushed into his home and forced him and his family to leave in nothing but their pajamas.

Dr. Frankl was immediately separated from his family. During the first few weeks of his imprisonment, he was starved, beaten, and forced to walk completely naked for miles from one concentration camp to another. To help him never forget how close he was to death, the Nazi guards gave him the task of removing dead bodies from the camp or shoveling the charred remains and ashes out of the gas chambers. His three years in concentration camps were marked by daily uncertainty whether he would live to see the next morning.

His mind would drift back to the warmth of his bed and the beauty of his wife and children in an effort to build a sense of sanity amid indescribable carnage and chaos. He had no idea that everyone he loved—his parents, brother, children, and wife—were all dead, some from the inhumane conditions of their concentration camps and others from the flames of gas ovens.

One day, while sitting alone and almost naked, with feet barely recognizable from frost bite, Dr. Frankl became aware of what he later called "the last of human freedoms." His Nazi captors could control his body, kill his friends and family, and make him do the most unthinkable acts for their pure entertainment, but Frankl discovered that in the midst of it all, he still retained the power to *choose* his attitude.

Reflecting on his time in Nazi captivity, Dr. Frankl said, "Everything can be taken from a man but one thing: the last of the human freedoms—to choose one's attitude in any given set of circumstances, to choose one's way."[1] The power to choose how we respond is a power that can never be taken; it can only be yielded.

Trying to answer the question "Why did this happen to me?" requires taking a set of facts, then filtering them through layers of personal interpretation. The struggle toward freedom from our past is so difficult because the way we answer our "why" determines how we see our role in the "what." The Bible tells us, "I can do all things through Christ who strengthens me" (Philippians 4:13 NKJV), but you can't put this principle into practice until you move from a place of powerlessness to a position of power. Your "why"—"Because

I deserved it" or "because I wasn't worthy of protection" or "because I wasn't worth loving"—may have led you down a path as destructive as my own, where you contemplated ending your life . . . or someone else's. But the hard truth is that why something happened doesn't change what happened. And what happened only has power over your life if you give it that power. As it was with Dr. Frankl, our challenge is to develop the ability to look at what happened to us and choose how we respond to it *going forward*.

> The way we answer our "why" determines how we see our role in the "what."

If your business partner embezzled your life savings and disappeared, their explanation won't suddenly restore your trust in them. If your spouse cheated on you, their explanation won't immediately heal your pain. If your sibling lied to you and turned your entire family against you, their explanation won't inspire you to invite them to brunch this weekend. Explanations don't have the power to heal us, but we put so much undue weight on the power of an explanation to do exactly that. Many of us go to great lengths to try to understand, but understanding isn't redemptive. And the truth is, most of the people who hurt us couldn't explain why they did it, anyway. Even after getting an "explanation" from Lee many years later, I didn't suddenly feel okay about what he did. It didn't erase the trauma and pain. Receiving an explanation for why we suffered never makes the impact of what we suffered disappear. And this is why it wasn't until I submitted my anger, disbelief, and fears to God through prayer, *with thanksgiving*, that I made peace with my "why."

Philippians 4:6 is one of my favorite Bible verses, but it's often misquoted. It says, "Do not be anxious about anything, but in every situation, by prayer and petition, with thanksgiving, present your requests to God." Many people skip over what I believe is the most important, life-giving part of this verse, the part that teaches us *how* to activate the power we need to combat anxiety, fear, and anger—gratitude. This verse tells us not to be anxious but instead to pray and seek God for what we need, with thanksgiving. As I grew into adulthood, my life began to change, and the toxic hold my past had on me weakened when I started going to God in prayer and thanking him for the good in my life, despite my pain. When I became intentionally and acutely aware of the goodness of God in my life, the "whys" of my past became less relevant to me. Gratefulness shifts our focus from the ashes of our past to the beautiful possibilities of our future.

> Gratefulness shifts our focus from the ashes of our past to the beautiful possibilities of our future.

We live our lives in a state of before, during, or after. If you aren't facing a challenge, wait. It's coming. If you're going through a difficult season, hold on. It will pass. If you recently overcame a difficulty, don't get too comfortable. "During" is on its way. The greatest challenge we face in life is that in the moment of our difficulty, it feels as if it is lasting an eternity. But the storm we're in is only temporary. The ever-changing nature of life means that no matter how desperate your situation may be at the moment, it's a season that will change at some point. When we assign more meaning and weight to our difficult season than it deserves, we may decide that it will "always be this way" when, in fact, the season may soon change. We just haven't experienced it yet.

If I'm honest, it isn't necessarily the facts of my trauma that have troubled me in my life. It was what those facts meant *to* me, *about* me, that troubled me most. It isn't what happened that breaks our spirit; it's what we *believe about what happened* that breaks our spirit. Resiliency, then, is what we build when we learn to become grateful for our "after," recognizing that we survived the "during" so God can release us from the grave clothes of our past.

> It isn't what happened that breaks our spirit; it's what we *believe about what happened* that breaks our spirit.

What remnants are you carrying in your own heart that are making it difficult to move forward? Were you bullied as a child and continue to see yourself through the lens of those hurtful remarks? What that person said about you was based on how they saw themselves. It isn't who you are. Did you endure the painful divorce of your parents and see yourself as the cause for their breakup? The decision they made had everything to do with them and the outlook they had on their marriage. It had nothing to do with you, even if they say it did.

Releasing the *why* in your life will require making the daily decision to leave the grave clothes of painful memories in the tomb of the past. No more blaming anyone for what happened. Especially not yourself. Whatever good exists in your life today is what deserves the energy, time, and attention you have given to the unexplainable past. And in releasing the why, you will be choosing your future. And choosing freedom. Let's discover how.

Chapter 4

Choosing Freedom

I placed my sixth-grade science book in my locker in exchange for my math book, and as I closed the door and turned to head to class, I heard the warm, familiar voice of my friend Betty calling my name.

"What's up, Nona?"

"Hey, Betty! About to head to math class."

"Did you practice those Lion King parts for Ms. Humphrey's class?"

"Not really. I've seen the movie, so I mostly know the songs."

"Hey, what are you doing Sunday? Want to come visit my church?"

"Church? What's that?"

Before that moment, believe it or not, I had never heard of church or God. My mom wasn't religious, and the only spiritual experience I can recall in retrospect was her taking me to her friend's house and watching them kneel before a pretty, tall black box and chant some strange words with closed eyes and bowed heads while clutching some beads in their clasped hands. I learned later in life that the practice was Buddhism, but I had no concept of a divine "other" as a child.

Mouth wide open in disbelief, she asked, "You don't know what church is? Quit playing!"

Through laughter I said, "I really don't. What is it?"

"Wow. Well, see if you can come with me and Mama on Sunday. We'll pick you up. It's not far from here."

"Okay. I'll ask my mom tonight."

I loved spending time with Betty and figured that if she was going, I would have fun. She was my second real friend. Before meeting her at the beginning of sixth grade, the only other friend I had was a girl in my fifth-grade class who was teased about her weight as much as I was. We had struck up a friendship on the playground one day when a boy who used to bully me called her fat and ugly, and she turned around, pushed him to the ground, and said, "Who you calling fat and ugly, looking like a fish? Your mama!" It was brilliant to me.

I wasn't the physically aggressive type. Even when kids would trip me or push me "on accident," I didn't retaliate. I just took it. Seeing her take that bully on in such fear-less fashion made me an instant fan. Seeing a girl who was even heavier than me stand her ground against people who picked on her for simply taking up space was mesmerizing. Kids avoided both of us, so we sat together at lunch, played together at recess, and became inseparable during my last year in elementary school. She lived across town and was bused to our school every day, a journey that took an hour each way. When it came time to go to middle school, her mom decided to put her in a school closer to them. I felt physically sick when she told me she wouldn't be with me in sixth grade. I knew I would never see my only friend again.

Betty and I met in chorus class and had to audition for parts in the school musical in front of everyone. We both had great voices and struck up a friendship around a shared love of music. My friendship with Betty was exactly what I needed. She had an easy sense of humor and could make any situation funny. She was kind and had a magnetic personality that effortlessly drew people to her, so I met many people by hanging out with her. When she invited me to go to church, I wasn't sure whether it was an event or a place, but whatever it was, getting out of the house on a weekend sounded like a dream.

"Mom?"

"What?"

"My friend Betty from school invited me to go to church with her Sunday. Can I go? Her mom will pick me up and bring me back."

She shrugged, filing through the mail without looking at me. "Okay."

I couldn't wait to tell Betty I could go with her to the church thing Sunday.

When Sunday came, I hopped into the back seat of their car with both curiosity and excitement. Less than fifteen minutes later, we pulled up to a building with a bunch of cars outside, and Betty's mom announced, "We're here." The church sign said Mandarin Church of God of Prophecy, and families of various sizes were climbing out of cars as we parked.

"Hey, Sister Kathy," one woman shouted at Betty's mom from across the parking lot.

"Good morning," she yelled back with a smile.

"Hey, Betty," a girl said as she walked by with her mom.

"Hey, Karissa," she said, waving.

The greetings continued in similar fashion as we made our way inside the building.

"Well, who do we have here?" a man said as I followed behind Betty and her mom.

"Hey, Brother Mike," Betty said. "This is my friend Nona from school. It's her first visit. Nona, this is Brother Mike. He leads the youth ministry."

There was a warmth and sincerity in Brother Mike's voice that immediately put me at ease. He was short and stout with a beard that made me think of the many pictures of Santa Claus I used to see in school around Christmastime.

"First visit? Well, welcome home, Nona," he said. "We're so glad you're here! I hope to see you next week in Sunday school. We have a class just for the youth and have a lot of fun together."

I smiled nervously and thanked him for inviting me, having no idea what he was talking about. But before I could get all my words out, a very tall woman walked up to me and gave me a big hug and said, "Good morning, sweetheart. Welcome!" She was followed by a line of people, both adults and youth, who offered bright smiles, warm hugs, and words of welcome. I was amazed. I didn't know any of those people, but by the time we sat down, I had been given more hugs and felt more love than I ever had in my life. I didn't know what church was, but whatever it was, I needed more of it.

———— ⚬⚬⚬ ————

We never know what people are battling when we meet them. We never know what people are carrying with them beneath the facade of their smile. When I walked through the doors of that church, I was an eleven-year-old survivor of two suicide attempts. I had been violated by my mom's boyfriend multiple times with her knowledge. I had been punched, slapped, and cursed at by my mom more times than I could count. I had been labeled a "problem child," "failure," and told by several teachers that I would never succeed. When I walked in those doors that Sunday morning, my soul was carrying more baggage than any child is equipped to handle on their own. And I was tired.

Have you ever been in such a place before? Where the person you portray is simply a character you play for others' benefit, but the real you, the one behind the costume of the successful executive, well-liked preacher, perfect mother, loving husband, or high-achieving college student, is exhausted from the charade? You wake up in the morning after a full eight hours of sleep, and you don't understand why you're not rested. But no amount of sleep will bring you rest when it's your soul that's tired.

> No amount of sleep will bring you rest when it's your soul that's tired.

In the book of Genesis, we find the story of God's creation of Adam. God formed Adam's body out of the dust of the ground and gave him life by breathing into Adam's lifeless body (Genesis 2:7). God could have created our bodies the same way he created everything else. He could have spoken it into existence. Instead, God formed our bodies out of the very earth he created, connecting us by design to the external world. God constructed us with a dual connection—to both the kingdom of nature through our body and the kingdom of God through our spirit. But at the intersection of our body and our spirit resides a third kingdom—the kingdom of the soul.

In the King James Version of Genesis 2:7, we are told that once God breathed life into Adam, he became a living soul. He was not a living body or a living spirit but instead became a living soul. Our soul is fundamentally who we are, and it's within our soul that our mind, will, and emotions reside. Because of its existence at the intersection of our body and our spirit, our soul is the filter through which we interpret the signals we receive through our body from the outside world and the signals we receive through our spirit from God. If our outside world is filled with neglect, abuse, and chaos, our soul filters those experiences and determines what we think about them, what we feel about them, and what we do about them. This is why the things that influence our soul are critically important to our lived reality.

God created us to be *spirit* led. He created us to look to him and him alone for guidance, assurance, and direction. God walked in the midst of Adam and Eve every day and regularly spoke with them while they stood naked and unashamed before him. They had nothing to hide from God, and he could trust them to trust him. But something changed after Adam and Eve yielded to the influence of the serpent and disobeyed God. Genesis 3:7 says, "Then the eyes of both of them were opened, and they realized they were naked; so they sewed fig leaves together and made coverings for themselves." Upon directing their attention to the fruit and viewing it as desirable, they ceased being spirit led and allowed their body, their flesh, to lead. When their souls received the signal from their bodies that the fruit was good, they thought about it, felt good about, then ate from the tree. And immediately their disobedience led them to cover their nakedness in shame.

When Adam and Eve looked to the outside world instead of to God for direction, assurance, and guidance, the first thing they experienced was a compulsion to cover themselves and hide. They believed the fig leaves covered their shame, but they weren't made to wear fig leaves; they were made to walk freely without shame. God told them that they would die the moment they disobeyed him. But the part of them that died that day was not their body; it was their receptivity to the spirit. Their spirit didn't die in the literal sense, but what died in them was the power their spirit exerted over their soul in order to lead their body.

All of us are born with a spirit that yearns to lead us the way God intended, but until we surrender our soul (mind, emotions, and will) to the spirit's control, we will naturally do what Adam and Eve did when confronted with a painful situation—cover up. For you, covering up might look like refusing to talk about your trauma, or perhaps you've learned to redirect conversations that head down that path by changing the subject. Maybe you have no problem talking about how you were raped by a person you thought was your friend or beaten by a person you thought was your lover, but you end the discussion with a simple, "But, hey, that was such a long time ago. I'm over it." Maybe you cover up the pain by avoiding family gatherings because that one person will be there. And maybe you've covered up by simply never telling anyone what happened to you in an effort to move on in your own power. None of these tactics can last over the long term because we weren't created to cover up our pain. We were created to live in freedom from our pain. Completely free.

> We weren't created to cover up our pain. We were created to live in freedom from our pain.

———— ∞ ————

Shortly after we settled into the church pews, a large man with a joyful grin stepped onto the stage and welcomed everyone to worship. He then asked everyone to bow their heads for prayer. I bowed my head slightly but kept my eyes open to see what was happening around me. After a few minutes of words of thanks to God, everyone said amen, and a lady played a piano. The man who opened in prayer went to a drum set and played along with her, and another man plucked a bass guitar. I don't remember what song they were singing, but I remember everyone stood up and started clapping and lifting their hands with so much enthusiasm that I stood and clapped too. There was an electricity in the room that made me feel light as I took in the scene of people exuberantly praising God.

Despite not knowing who God was, I could tell the church people really liked him. They sang songs about him, and during one particular song, people danced in the aisles. It was both a spectacle and an experience at the same time. After the lively music, the musicians played a slow song that had such a sad melody that it immediately resonated with me. As they played, something welled up within me, and tears formed at the corners of my eyes. It was a song of worship to a God I didn't know, but I was so impacted by the music that it still moved me. Deeply. As I looked around the room, I noticed other people shedding tears, with heads bowed and arms outstretched. I wondered whether they were also nursing pain as I was, but although I will never know what was in their hearts and minds at that moment, I will never forget how being in a room full of people who were so vulnerable made me feel safe to be vulnerable too.

The music continued to play softly as an unassuming man walked up to the platform from the front row. He had a book in his hand and placed it on the podium. He prayed like the first man did, but never asked us to bow our heads. Instinctively, I knew to do so. After he said amen, everyone else said amen and took their seats. As I sat down, he said a few words of welcome and asked whether there were any first-time visitors. I looked around and saw a few people stand up, so I stood as well. He expressed additional words of welcome, and the people sitting near me reached out to give me more hugs. When we sat down again, he asked everyone to turn to Psalm 68. Thankfully, Betty's mom opened a book that was sitting in the seat-back pocket in front of us and handed it to me with a gentle finger pointing to the section he had indicated. He read the Scripture passage, and I followed along until we came across words that hit me squarely in the heart. "A father of the fatherless, and a judge of the widows, *is* God in his holy habitation" (Psalm 68:5 KJV).

A father of the fatherless? That's me. How did he know that?

I don't remember the rest of what he said that day, but I remember staring at those words over and over again. In my times of greatest anguish and despair, I would cry out for my father to help me. I remember many nights when I called aloud for my dad through tears, asking him to come back. To read at that moment that God is a father to the fatherless was like hearing my own father's voice speaking to me. I wanted to know more about this "God." I wanted to know more about him being my father. I asked Betty's mom whether I could keep the book to read more, and she said yes. After the service that day, Betty and her mom introduced me to the man who had spoken up front, and I learned his name was Brother Larry Lowery. He introduced his wife as Sister Susan, and I realized she was the woman who had been playing the piano. Their genuine warmth was comforting, and I immediately felt as though they loved me without even knowing me.

When I got home that day, I ran to my room and read Psalm 68 in its entirety. Then I went to the table of contents to see what the other parts of the book were called. It looked like a bunch of people's names, but many of the names in the first part of the book were strange, so I decided to stay in the Psalms and started reading Psalm 1. Because I spent so much time alone, I had developed a love for reading at an early age, and books had become my escape from the chaos. But I found this book hard to understand. The words seemed as though they came from a different time or place, so when I got to school the next day, I told Betty I needed help understanding what it was saying.

"Oh, you probably have an old version. Like the King James or something."

"The what? Old version? What do you mean?"

"You probably need a version like I have. It reads easier. Like in plain English."

"Oh, okay. How can I get one of those?"

"I'll let Mama know. She'll get you one, or there's probably one at the church."

I returned to church the following week with Betty and her mom and was grateful for a New King James Bible that read much easier. The youth ministry leader, Brother Mike, stopped me after the service and asked whether I was coming to Sunday school the following week, but I told him it all depended on Betty's mom, since she was my ride. He asked where I lived, and when I told him my neighborhood, he said, "That's along our drive to church. My family can pick you up if you want to come." I had felt so much love from Brother Mike and his family that I said, "That would be great," and told Betty's mom about the change. She smiled and said she was glad I wanted to attend Sunday school. When I attended the following week, I found myself in a classroom with others my age. Brother Mike taught in a way that invited discussion, so I asked a lot of questions about God and Jesus and prayer and faith and soaked in the answers.

After a few Sundays of my questions, Brother Mike stopped me in the hallway after Sunday school and asked me whether Jesus was Lord of my life. I gave him a puzzled look.

"Are you saved, Nona?"

"Saved? I don't know what that is. I guess not."

"You seem to have a natural hunger for God's Word. You ask great questions. I think the spirit of God is working in your life and calling you closer to Jesus."

"You do? What does that mean?"

"It simply means that God has his hand on you. The Bible says that no one can come to the Father unless the Spirit draws them, and from everything I can see, the Spirit is drawing you to God. That's why you have so many questions. So now the question is: Do you want to follow Jesus and make him Lord of your life?"

"Well, yes. What do I have to do?"

"We're going to pray together for Jesus to become your Savior. But more than praying for Jesus to *become* your Savior, you're going to have to *make* him your Savior by choosing to follow him every day, choosing to honor him with your life and every decision you make. Can you do that?"

"I can try. I want to try."

"Okay. Let me grab my wife, and we can find a place to pray you through your decision."

When we found his wife, he told her what he wanted us to pray about, and she smiled so big that I could see all her teeth.

She hugged me tight and said, "Nona, this is the best decision you will ever make in your life. And I'm so honored to be part of it."

With that, the three of us walked back to the youth classroom, and they prayed for me and with me. I accepted Jesus as Lord of my life that day, at twelve years old. We prayed that God would forgive me for my sins as I forgave those who sinned against me. And I immediately thought about Mom and Lee. So much of the pain, anger, frustration, and distress I was carrying was because of them. Yet in submitting my heart and life to the Lord, I became aware of the need to forgive my offenders, not because they were blameless but because a blameless Savior had died for me *and them*. It was not a suggestion that I forgive; it was a command. But how? How could I forgive the people who *continued* to hurt me?

In a case where our offender is nameless, faceless, or physically removed, we can sometimes move on more quickly. If we had our identity stolen by an unidentified hacker somewhere in the world, we would feel violated and angry, but it's difficult to channel anger at something invisible. But when our offender has a face, name, address, job, hobbies, and lives near us or remains connected to us, it's far more challenging to move past the pain. And if our offender continues to be part of our daily lives, heaven help us. If you have a child with that cheating boyfriend or see the cousin who stole your wife at family reunions or your best friend remains close with the business partner who ruined your credit, what do you do then? How do you "release the why" when the sound of your offender's voice rings loudly in your ears? Especially when that voice has never carried the words "I'm sorry." What do you do?

You choose freedom.

——— ⌾ ———

"He never even said he was sorry."

"She knew she did me wrong, but she kept acting like everything was okay."

"I feel like I could move on with my life if I just knew he was sorry about what he did."

As children, we're taught to say we're sorry when our actions cause harm to others, and as we grow into adults, it becomes ingrained in us to expect people to express regret when they do something hurtful. This is human, and the desire to make things right, to even the scales, is natural. But you can probably think of times you said I'm sorry when you really weren't, just to appease someone. We often place a high value on receiving an apology after we've been wronged because we believe hearing I'm sorry will bring closure to our pain. Many of us wait days, weeks, months, or years for our offender's remorse to show as a way of restoring a sense of justice. And that's the problem.

An apology isn't an indicator of regret; it's a function of social conditioning. People apologize because it's the right thing to do, not because it evens the scales of offense. The myth of the apology is that it has the power to change a situation if spoken with sincerity. The *reality* of the apology is that it has no intrinsic power to heal the person receiving it. An apology is like a picture of a car—it has the appearance of something that can take you somewhere, but it's nothing more than a representation of what actually can. What we need is not the appearance of freedom; we need *actual* freedom. But what can take us there?

It's natural to be angry when someone hurts us. You don't even have to exert extra effort. You simply yield to the natural feelings that come from being slighted. It's as easy as inhaling your next breath. You aren't sitting there concentrating on breathing. You aren't afraid of going to sleep because your brain might forget to breathe. Instead, you breathe without worry because breathing is controlled at an automatic level. Decide to stay underwater for five minutes, however, and you have an entirely different challenge on your hands. We don't get medals for breathing, but there are real-life competitions to see how long people can hold their breath. Why? Because holding your breath *isn't* natural and requires strength. Similarly, reversing the natural inclination toward anger when we are hurt requires strength. Divine strength.

If you've never run a mile before, it would probably be unwise to try to run a marathon. Your body won't be conditioned for it, and you will end up injured and miserable. Just as a race requires physical conditioning, rising from past pain will require soul conditioning. It will require exercising authority over your thoughts, emotions, and actions in ways you may have never tried before. This means we all begin our healing journey weak and needing a strength-training regimen. And our souls get stronger the same way our bodies get stronger—by doing that which is unnatural. It's unnatural to run long distances and lift heavy weights, but building our cardiovascular and musculoskeletal strength requires both.

For you, one of the greatest tests of your strength will be exercising the power to forgive someone who never even apologized for hurting you. Forgiving someone who never seeks forgiveness is unnatural. It's like entering a breath-holding competition when the longest you've held your breath is the time it takes to exhale your last one. And equally difficult is choosing to forgive someone who has apologized, but you don't feel you can accept their apology. Maybe they weren't sincere. Maybe they apologized only because they got caught, not because they hurt you. Maybe their apology was used in a twisted way to blame *you* for their actions. When I was in the sixth grade, Lee apologized for hurting me after watching an episode of Maury Povich's show that featured victims of sexual abuse. But his apology didn't make my nightmares go away. And it didn't make me trust him. My mom has semi-apologized to me, with a "but." She told me she was sorry, "But I needed help paying the bills." Another time she told me she was sorry, "But it wouldn't have happened if you would have kept your legs closed."

Whether the person who hurt you never apologized to you or they offered an unacceptable apology, it won't cancel the damage they did. It can be canceled only through the power of forgiveness. And the good news is, *that* power is perfectly within reach.

⸺⸺∞⸺⸺

In February and July 1985, two Birmingham area fast-food managers were killed in separate armed robberies. The survivor of a third attempted armed robbery was brought in for questioning and, when presented with photos of potential suspects, picked twenty-nine-year-old Anthony Ray Hinton from the options. Hinton was arrested and charged with the murders despite his boss testifying that he was at work during the time of the crimes. The media immediately cast Hinton, a young black man living with his mother in rural Alabama, as guilty. His picture became synonymous with the crime even though it took two years before the case went to trial, and the only evidence offered at the trial were four crime-scene bullets that were said to have matched Hinton's mother's gun. No fingerprints or eyewitness testimony were provided, and Hinton was convicted of each murder and sentenced to death. Alabama rejoiced at getting such a "lowlife" off the street, but the fact that Hinton was black and the jury of his "peers" was white meant the racial overtones of his case were as clear as the eye could see. Although he was carried off to prison, he maintained his plea of not guilty.

Hinton's death sentence placed him in solitary confinement, where he would spend much of his thirty years in prison smelling the burning flesh of inmates being executed in the nearby electric chair. The rancid smell was a constant reminder that death was just outside his jail cell, and when he asked a guard whether there was anything that could be done about it, the guard laughed and said, "You'll get used to it. Next year or one of these days, somebody's going to be smelling you just the same."[1] Ten years into his sentence, Hinton's case was picked up by the Equal Justice Initiative, and they vowed to fight all the way to the Supreme Court on his behalf. Then, seventeen years into his life sentence, in September 2002, Hinton's mother died. She had maintained monthly visits to see her son up until the time of her death. She never lost faith in his innocence, and her unwavering belief in him helped sustain him during the lengthy legal battle that was to come. After her death, the memory of the day she broke down in court when he was sentenced pained him every time he thought of her.

Twelve years later, in 2014, the US Supreme Court ruled that Hinton's original defense lawyer was "constitutionally deficient" and remanded his case to the lower court for retrial. The court cited that his defense lawyer had hired a one-eyed, ill-trained civil engineer as the ballistics expert. In 2015, when forensic experts in the Jefferson County district attorney's office failed to match the crime scene bullets to Hinton's mother's gun, the office dropped the case. On April 3, 2015, he was released from prison, and all charges against him were dropped. In sharing his thoughts on the injustice, Hinton said, "Since my release, not one prosecutor, or state attorney general, or anyone having anything to do with my conviction has apologized. I doubt they ever will. I forgive them. I made a choice after the first difficult few weeks of freedom, when everything was new and strange and the world didn't seem to make sense to me. I chose to forgive. I chose to stay vigilant to any signs of anger or hate in my heart. They took thirty years of my life. If I couldn't forgive, if I couldn't feel joy, that would be like giving them the rest of my life. The rest of my life is mine."[2]

⸺⸻∞⸻⸺

Many people refuse to forgive their offender because they believe that person doesn't "deserve" it. But forgiveness is misunderstood. While forgiveness is something we extend *to* our offender, forgiveness is never *about* our offender.

Forgiveness is the gift we give *ourselves* by no longer allowing our past to control our future.

I frequently travel for business and speaking engagements, and I always travel as light as possible. Whether I'm gone for a day or a week, I take only a carry-on suitcase unless the occasion truly calls for more than I can pack in it. When I walk into any airport in the world, the first thing I observe are the types of people walking in with me. Some are like me, traveling light and strolling casually to security screening. But others

> Forgiveness is the gift we give *ourselves* by no longer allowing our past to control our future.

carry multiple pieces of large luggage, struggling to keep everything together. This latter group of people are living metaphors for the way many of us look to God—walking through life burdened with luggage, filled with anger, bitterness, and grudges from past pain.

Just as airports require you to keep your luggage with you at all times, an unforgiving heart requires the same. It forces you to stay attached to the painful reminders of what your offender did, and it keeps a growing list of offenses caused by the intentional or unintentional actions of others. Forgiveness is like a skycap who sees you struggling with your luggage and offers to take it for you. For free. And Jesus is that person. Matthew 11:28 finds Jesus instructing us to "come to me, all you who are weary and burdened, and I will give you rest." But Jesus can't give rest to a heart that refuses to forgive.

There's a common misconception that forgiving someone somehow gives them a pass. For a long time, I felt that way about my mom and Lee. As much as I loved my church and the Lord, there were times when my pastor would preach about forgiveness and I would think, "Yeah, easy for you to say. You don't know what I've been through." But here's the catch: people who haven't apologized to you aren't sitting around stewing over what they did. They've moved on with their lives. They're sleeping well at night. And the only one thinking about what they did is you. Forgiveness isn't about letting *them* off the hook. Forgiveness is letting someone off the hook and discovering it was you.

Hebrews 12:15 says, "See to it that no one falls short of the grace of God and that no bitter root grows up to cause trouble and defile many." Forgiveness isn't about only us, it's about the people we love and how we show up for them. When we allow pain to fester, it doesn't stay trapped on the inside. It begins to affect the way we treat other people. The danger in this is that we create a cycle of pain in which we move from being the victim to being the per-petrator. It is commonly said that "hurt people hurt people," and I agree. The hurt we don't release to God becomes the hurt we release on others. Maybe you throw your-self into work so you don't have time to think about your past, but the sacrifice you make is the time your family so very much wants to spend with you. Maybe you con-stantly criticize your children no matter how hard they try because your own identity was fractured and you take your value from how well others perceive you as a parent. Maybe your significant other is on the brink of leaving you because your anger has made them feel unsafe. In all these cases and more, our hurt simply hurts the people we care most about.

> Forgiveness is letting someone off the hook and discovering it was you.

Choosing freedom requires intentionality. It requires identifying the person who hurt you and being willing to release yourself from the need to punish them for hurting you. It's a daily practice that must begin with prayer and confession to God about how you feel. Maybe you wish they were dead. Maybe you wish someone would hurt them. Maybe you wish they had never been born. You must confess those thoughts to God. And once you confess, you must surrender to the perfect will of God and begin to pray for them. Pray that God would make their heart tender to the pain they have caused you so they don't hurt anyone else, and pray that God would orchestrate their life to bring them face-to-face with the offense they caused you. But whether that happens or not, you can pray for God to give you the grace to release your offender from your wrath, because until you release them from your wrath, the past is still in your present.

Meditate on the Word of God to keep your soul under the influence of your spirit because your body, your flesh, will resist the unnatural work of forgiveness. It will want to comfortably stretch out in the natural anger that comes so easily. Instead, make the following verses your daily declarations until the words are imprinted on your soul:

Romans 12:18: "If it is possible, as far as it depends on you, live at peace with everyone."

Matthew 6:15: "If you do not forgive others their sins, your Father will not forgive your sins."

Colossians 3:13: "Bear with each other and forgive one another if any of you has a grievance against someone. Forgive as the Lord forgave you."

Matthew 11:29: "Take my yoke upon you and learn from me, for I am gentle and humble in heart, and you will find rest for your souls."

Ephesians 4:31–32: "Get rid of all bitterness, rage and anger, brawling and slander, along with every form of malice. Be kind and compassionate to one another, forgiving each other, just as in Christ God forgave you."

As you build the muscle of your soul by exercising your forgiveness muscles through the Word of God, you will discover a freedom that can be attributed only to the power of the Holy Spirit working through you. And once you learn how to extend God's grace to others, you will discover the importance of extending his grace to the one who needs it most—you.

Chapter 5

Never beyond Repair

"Get out of my house!"

I was twelve years old and reading in my bedroom on a Saturday morning when Mom burst in with fire in her eyes, cursing and screaming at me. It was so sudden and unexplainable that I thought I was dreaming. I could usually sense when Mom was going to have an episode, because she would start by talking to herself under her breath and walking rapidly around the house. When I saw those signs, I knew to find a quiet place to lie low and stay out of her line of sight. But that day I hadn't seen her and didn't know she was in a rage first thing in the morning.

"What? I don't have anywhere to go," I said in shock.

"I don't care where you go! Just get out!"

"What did I do? Why are you so angry? Why are you doing this?"

I apparently didn't wash the dishes the night before. Something as simple as that was enough to spark the entirety of her fury for hours. Washing the dishes before I went to bed was a customary part of my nighttime routine, so forgetting to do it one time and being told to get out of the house left me confused.

"I'm sick of you! I never wanted you! Get out of my house! And don't take anything I bought you!"

I stared at her, trying to make sense of what she was saying to me, but I could barely hear the profanity she was throwing my way over the rapid-fire thoughts racing through my mind. Where could I go? Who could help me? I was barely in middle school, so how could I take care of myself? Why did she want me gone? Why did Lee get to stay? Why was I so worthless to her? At one point she walked toward me, and I knew that was the signal to move, so I jumped up and slipped past her just as her fist made its way onto my back. I headed for the front door and ran out once I reached it. I was wearing my pajamas and socks but kept walking to the front of our neighborhood. Once I got there, I did the only thing I could think to do—I started walking toward church.

As the church came into view, I remembered one of the families that lived in a trailer nearby and walked up to their front door and knocked. Thankfully, the mom was home. She answered the door with a big smile, then a look of bewilderment as she took in the full sight of me in my pajamas and dirty socks.

"Nona, why are you out here dressed like that?"

"My mom made me leave."

"Huh? Leave? Your house? Oh no! Come on in. Let me fix you a sandwich."

As I sat at the tiny kitchen table, she walked into a side room and returned with a pair of sweatpants and a shirt.

"Here are some clean clothes. Go ahead and put these on. The kids are out with their dad fishing. What size shoe do you wear?"

"Eight."

"Okay. I'm going to run to Payless to get you some shoes. Are you okay here until I get back?"

"Yes, ma'am."

"All right. The television is in the room over there, and you can help yourself to anything in the fridge. Make yourself comfortable, honey. I'm so sorry your day started like this."

I watched as she made her way out the front door, and as soon as the door closed behind her, I felt something wet on my cheeks. I had started crying but didn't even realize it. The many years I had spent training myself not to feel anything had left me numb to the pain alive within me. Even when the pain tried to come out in the form of tears, I taught myself not to allow too many to fall, so I wiped them on the back of my hand and looked down at my uneaten sandwich. I had no desire to eat it. Food had become my medicine over the years, but I was feeling a kind of sickness that not even food could help. I felt heart sickness. Lee had told me that if I ever told Mom what he did to me that she would get rid of me, and here I was, discarded like a piece of trash. He was right.

The Bible says that we are fearfully and wonderfully made, meaning we were crafted with loving care and precision by the hands of God. But when people we look to for affirmation of our worth treat us as though we're expendable to them, it crushes our soul and fractures our identity. I didn't have the language for it then, but looking back on the day my mom put me out, I now realize that the sickness I felt in my heart was the pain of being disposable. Although I had a relationship with Jesus by that time and had been under enough teaching to know God loved and cared for me, there was something deeply painful about having the one who brought me into the world tell me to my face that

> When people we look to for affirmation of our worth treat us as though we're expendable to them, it crushes our soul and fractures our identity.

she didn't want me. She had said it many times before, but when she said it that day *and* told me to get out of the house, it broke me yet again.

To this day my greatest struggle has been the pain of being disposable to people. It's such a raw area that I once told a guy at the outset of our relationship that, if his intentions weren't good, to please not play with my heart. I told him I couldn't take being hurt, and he assured me he would never hurt me. But not long after assuring me he wouldn't hurt me, that's *exactly* what he did. He was enamored of the idea of me—the beautiful, accomplished girl who other guys wanted. But he discarded the *real* me—the person who needed love and support because of deeply rooted insecurities. My mom was the same way. She felt personal triumph for my accomplishments and how good they made her look, but when it came to nurturing and protecting *me*, the person, I was expendable. This type of treatment bruises your spirit and makes you question whether you're even worthy of the kind of love your heart thirsts for. And you can begin to think something is wrong with you. You can begin to believe *you* are defective.

Maybe this has been you. You know what the Word of God says about you in your head; but your head isn't the problem. You have a head full of Bible verses affirming your value in Christ and can rattle them off to a friend in their own time of insecurity. You have a head full of teachings from empowerment conferences around the country and share quotes on social media to encourage other people. But a head full of information can't help you when it's your heart that's the problem. Your head knows what the Bible *says* about you, but your heart sees what the person *does* to you, and the conflict between the two makes you sometimes doubt whether God *really* has a purpose and plan for you. As I sat alone at the kitchen table in the trailer that day, I prayed for God to help me see what he was doing in my life, because I couldn't figure it out. I was twelve years old and couldn't envision anything more than what I was feeling, so I asked God to help me see the truth in his Word. I had memorized two passages of Scripture by then,

> A head full of information can't help you when it's your heart that's the problem.

Psalm 1 and Psalm 23, so I prayed using those Scriptures because words escaped me.

"Lord, I don't want to walk in the counsel of the ungodly or stand in the way of sinners or sit in the seat of scorners. I delight in your law and meditate in it day and night. You plant me like a tree by the rivers of water so I can bring forth fruit in my season. Lord . . . when is my season? I can't see it right now. I can't feel it right now. You are my Shepherd, and I know I should not want, but God, I want peace. I need peace. My heart hurts. I need you to restore my soul and to lead me in the paths of righteousness for your name's sake. I feel like I'm walking through the valley of the shadow of death right now, but you are with me. You always have comforted me. You've never forsaken me. I trust your Word; you are preparing a table before me in the presence of those who hurt me. Because of you, goodness and mercy will follow me all the days of my life. And I promise I will dwell in your house forever. Amen."

It was in that trailer, with nothing but my pain sharing space with me, that God helped me begin to realize how deep his grace reaches into the depths of our pain. As I prayed his Word, I felt the spirit of God envelop me with the assurance that he had the situation under control. His Word became the mirror I desperately needed in order to see myself through his eyes. When we look at our situations through our natural eyes, they can make us feel helpless and hopeless because we have no power in and of ourselves to change them. Yet when we look at our situation through the lens of God's Word, we come to recognize that our broken places are never beyond his reach and therefore are never beyond his repair. We need God to help us see ourselves the way he sees us because our brokenness distorts the reflection we see in our mind's eye.

> While forgiveness is necessary to release our offender from our future, grace is necessary to release ourselves from our past.

While forgiveness is necessary to release our offender from our future, grace is necessary to release ourselves from our past. The word *grace* appears many times throughout the Bible to describe the spiritual healing we receive when we entrust our lives to God through faith in Jesus. Ephesians 2:8–9 says, "It is by grace you have been saved, through faith—and this not from yourselves, it is the gift of God—not by works, so that no one can boast." Grace rescues us from the pain of our past. Grace reclaims our identity as chosen by God. Grace restores our value as precious in his sight. Grace reestablishes the relationship that was severed in the garden of Eden. Grace is the supernatural power that allows us to see ourselves and our situations as God does.

We invite God's grace into our lives when we surrender our wills to his Word and submit our pain to his purpose.

———⊗⊗⊗———

"Ms. Brown, can you have Nona come to the main office?" the loudspeaker crackled into my sixth-grade science class.

"Sure," Ms. Brown replied. "Nona, take the hall pass."

I made my way to the main office, unsure of why I was going there, but when I rounded the corner, I saw my mom sitting in the waiting area. I hadn't seen her in at least a month and didn't know what she was doing there. When she saw me, she stood up and thanked the receptionist before telling me to come outside. She looked unusually tired, as if she hadn't been sleeping.

"Why do I have to come to this school to talk to you? You haven't even called me! I haven't heard from you one time!"

I was stunned, unsure of what to say when we both knew the truth.

"You . . . told me to . . . leave."

"Well, you were being disrespectful. You can come home after school today."

"But what should I tell the family I've been staying with?"

"Nothing! You don't need to tell them anything. I should press charges on them for not calling to tell me where you were! They go to that church you been going to?"

"Yes."

"Well, you ain't going there no more. Any church that would think it's okay not to have a child call their mother is dead wrong."

My heart dropped. "Huh? No. I can't leave. They're my . . . my . . . family," I said, looking down at the ground.

"No! I'm your family. I'm your mother. You can tell all those church people to butt out of our business. I'll see you at home later. I have to go to work."

I was dumbfounded and devastated. My mind was once again racing, and I wasn't sure what to make of what had just happened. My church was the one place that had provided a constant stream of hope and encouragement. And the family that let me stay with them became like family to me. We ate dinner together, prayed together, played in their large yard together, and I always felt as though they had my best interests in mind. But now my mom was suddenly coming back on the scene and taking it all away.

I went home after school to find Lee sitting in the family room drinking a beer and watching television. He looked up and winked at me when I walked in, saying, "Welcome back," as if I had just stepped out for a few minutes to get the mail. I walked to my room and set my things down, then sat on my bed with a heavy heart. During my month away, I had started to dream of a future. I had decided I wanted to become a doctor, even though I had no clue what that required. I had begun to see myself with options and opportunities because with the other family, we talked about things such as college. I had never heard the word *college* in Mom's house, mostly because her third-grade education meant she was unable to tell me anything about it. But while I was away, I began to think about what I wanted to do after I graduated from high school.

The thought of graduating from high school and moving away for college was exhilarating. If being in another home for only a month could give me an entirely new perspective on life, I knew moving away permanently would be life changing. So as I sat on my bed that first day back and reflected on my time away from home, I was inspired to set a new goal for myself—graduate from high school and never come back. I felt as though part of me died the day Mom put me out, but as I reflected on my time away, I smiled at the recognition that she thought she was hurting me, but instead, God was using her to help me. *Grace* has been defined as "unmerited favor," and for so

> That which was meant to leave you broken can be used by God to make you brave.

long I thought my life was beyond the reach of God's grace. Yet God used that church and that family to show that his grace can find us in the most painful of circumstances, and that which was meant to leave you broken can be used by God to make you brave.

Marian Hatcher had a corporate job in finance and was married with five children in her thirties when the pain from her past interrupted her promising future. She had been molested as a child, and her outward success simply masked an internal brokenness that stayed with her. When her husband started to beat her, feeling she had nowhere to turn, she turned to drugs. "Crack cocaine brought me to my knees. . . . That drug became the love of my life and told me it was okay to leave my children."[1]

To escape her pain, she sold her body to keep up with her insatiable need to get high. She eventually started working for pimps so she could stay high and drunk without having to face the fact that she had left her family. She was missing for almost two years before she was arrested and sent to Cook County Jail. It was then that her sobriety forced her to come face-to-face with a past she had been avoiding her entire life.

The judge sentenced her to three to seven years in prison, but instead, she ended up serving four months in an area women's drug treatment program. It was there she was given the tools needed to dig into her soul to dredge up the shame that she had been covering up with multiple marriages, drugs, and prostitution. After doing the hard work of uncovering her pain and making peace with her past, she realized she had a calling that was bigger than herself. Her pain had purpose.

She began working with the county sheriff to shift the way they pursued trafficking victims, helping change their philosophy from going after the women who *sell* sex to going after the people who *buy* it. And her work didn't stop there. Hatcher teamed up with justice officials at the national level to begin speaking out and educating people about the issue of human trafficking across the US. In 2016 she became one of only twenty individuals to receive the President's Volunteer Service Award from President Obama in recognition of her tireless work and impact.

In recounting the arrest that catalyzed the change in her life's trajectory, she said, "Angels with handcuffs brought me to Cook County Jail."[2] A woman who had numbed herself with drugs and alcohol to escape her pain was now using her story to help others escape their own.

The pain we keep trapped inside doesn't stay buried; it seeps out through our decisions and relationships. I can't tell you how many unwise decisions I made because of unresolved hurt. I am sad to say I've had both platonic and romantic relationships in which I gave too much of myself when it wasn't safe to do so. They were the fruit of unresolved hurt stirring my emotions. I simply wanted to be wanted by someone, *anyone*. The wrong one. Perhaps you can relate to this. Maybe you look over your shoulder and see a trail of past decisions and relationships that you aren't proud of. Yet at the core of those mistakes was the hope that you would find the comfort, security, and validation you needed. That car you bought in an effort to impress people but couldn't afford got repossessed. That woman you gave your heart to despite the red flags that she was going to be unfaithful. The old boyfriend you reconnected with on social media because you and your husband have been getting into arguments.

> The pain we keep trapped inside doesn't stay buried; it seeps out through our decisions and relationships.

I want to offer you the truth that no matter what you've done and no matter how much shame you have carried because of it, you are never beyond repair. In Christ Jesus we have immediate and direct access to redemption power, the power to write a new story. Every day God is calling to you and me to write that new story with the grace he gives us in the gift of life. Many people planned to see today's date and didn't make it. But you did. And you did on purpose. God wants to build a testimony for others out of the ashes of your past, but only you can let him. God's grace is extended to you right now, and he is inviting you to commune with him so he can work in your life.

Take this time to get before God and receive his grace by verbally confessing the ways your pain may have directed your decisions and relationships against his perfect will. Maybe you've been sleeping with multiple people under the guise of sexual liberation when in truth you're afraid of giving someone access to your heart. Your decision is driven by a fear of vulnerability. Maybe you've allowed your boyfriend to abuse you under the guise of trying to help him heal from past relational hurts. You say he's just angry because his old girlfriend left him, so you excuse his behavior. But in truth you're afraid of what letting him go would mean about yourself. You hang on to the relationship because being single makes you feel you're unlovable.

Part of the work God wants to do in you and me requires getting honest with why we accept what we accept and why we think so little of ourselves. Nothing you do could make God love you any more, and nothing you do could make God love you any less. No matter what others' lives look like, we're all fighting a private battle that nobody knows about. So you no longer have to think that your brand of brokenness is too much for God's grace to handle. He wants all of you. Every part. Piece. And scrap. Because only the hand of your Creator can put you back together again.

And when he puts you back together, he expects you to live out *your* unique purpose.

Chapter 6

Run Your Own Race

Something changed inside me after my mom made me stop attending my church and I could no longer see the family that took me in when she kicked me out. I was angry, but the discussions I'd had with that family about college channeled my anger into ambition. That family didn't have a lot of money, but what the parents couldn't give in material possessions, they gave in inspiration. They would sit around the dinner table and talk with their children about what they were going to be when they grew up, emphasizing the importance of good grades as the ticket to college and a better life. They encouraged their children to become doctors or lawyers so they could create a better life for their future families. Those dinnertime conversations inspired me to imagine what I could be when I grew up if I worked hard and made good grades. Discovering the *possibility* of better is often what helps us become better ourselves.

> Discovering the *possibility* of better is often what helps us become better ourselves.

—— ∞∞∞ ——

"Ms. Chastain, can I come back during lunch and work through a few of these math problems with you? I want to make sure I understand them before I try them at home by myself tonight."

My sixth-grade math teacher looked at me with both puzzlement and excitement and said, "Of course, Nona! My door is always open. I'll see you during lunch."

I had learned halfway through fifth grade that there were two tracks for students in middle school—regular classes or advanced classes. My fifth-grade teacher didn't recommend me for the advanced track, so when I started middle school, I did the bare minimum because I didn't see the point of putting in extra effort. I didn't study for tests and often turned in half-completed homework. I was mostly a C student who occasionally managed a B- by the grace of God. It wasn't until those dinnertime conversations with the family that took me in that I thought about the future. Setting my sights on college made me realize that coasting wasn't going to cut it.

When I returned home, the dysfunction there no longer saddened me. It motivated me to pay attention in class so I could leave for college after graduation. I asked questions when I didn't understand something and made homework a priority every night. Since Mom's third-grade education rendered her unable to help me with my schoolwork, I would notate problems I wasn't able to do on my own and ask my teacher for help before turning in an assignment. As I applied myself in the classroom, I unearthed a passion for learning that suddenly made school exciting for me. I developed a deep love of science and math because of the predictability, a juxtaposition to the unpredictability of my life at the time. I loved how formulas and equations created order out of chaos, and once I understood how to work a problem or experiment, I learned I could apply that model across similar problems and experiments to arrive at a conclusive correct answer. I also excelled in English because I was able to quickly learn even the most complex vocabulary with ease and became a celebrated writer.

Halfway through my sixth-grade year, my teachers got together, unbeknownst to me, and decided to promote me to all advanced classes. They felt as though my intellectual capacity was greater than the level of work being offered in the standard classes I was in.

"Nona, we think you have a lot of potential," said my science teacher, Mrs. Mathis. "We're going to put you in advanced classes and give you more of a challenge. Are you up for that?"

I had been told I would amount to nothing but failure.

I had been told I had no future.

I had been told I didn't have what it takes.

But that day I heard something entirely different.

Hearing my teacher say those words made me suddenly feel ten feet tall. The idea that my teachers saw something good in me after all those years of being told something was wrong with me swelled my heart. But my boost of confidence was short lived. Thoughts began to fill my mind that maybe they somehow had made a mistake and I wasn't ready for advanced classes. Throughout elementary school and the first half of sixth grade, I had always felt "less than" because I compared myself with the kids in gifted and advanced classes. Although I had tested gifted at a young age, I was told I wasn't going to be placed in the elementary gifted program because of my behavior. When my fifth-grade teacher didn't recommend me for sixth-grade advanced classes, I felt even more inadequate and secretly envied the "advanced kids" as they sat together during lunch. But when God spoke through Mrs. Mathis that day, he used her to do more than promote me to more challenging classes; he used her to affirm my value. Her words were like a balm to my weary soul.

Making the transition to advanced classes in the middle of my sixth-grade school year was difficult. I not only had to acclimate to new, accelerated academic material quickly, but I also had to find a way to fit in with a group of kids who had been treated as royals for most of their existence. The first day I stepped into advanced English, a group of girls looked at me disdainfully and whispered while periodically glancing my way, laughing. I felt like an unwelcome guest in their house for several weeks, but when my report card came out lined with As and Bs, the mean girls figured I might not be as much of an impostor as they thought, and they gradually stopped singling me out for their passive-aggressive stare-whisper-stare-whisper sessions. I, on the other hand, wasn't comforted by my grades. I still felt as though I didn't belong.

Years of being told I was a "problem child" had shaped my understanding of who I was and my limitations, so when I sat in those advanced classes with the sixth-grade "golden children," I couldn't help but think I was there by mistake. When those kids spoke of vacationing at Club Med for spring break, I didn't know what a vacation was and thought Club Med was a hospital of some sort. When they spoke about their moms being housewives and their dads being doctors, lawyers, or business owners, I couldn't imagine telling them my mom was a home health aide with a third-grade education and a live-in boyfriend getting a disability check. So instead, I learned not to say anything at all. I listened, nodded, and smiled. Their ordinary life was extraordinary to me.

Being the only black girl in all my advanced classes didn't make things any easier either because several of the kids said things like "blacks aren't that smart" and "the only black person who's ever been in our house is our maid." To them, black people were "inferior." I heard things such as that so regularly that I began to wonder whether I was there only because of my race or whether I was part of some "diversity project." I couldn't conceive of how I ended up in the same classes as the kids who wore Ralph Lauren sweater-vests and hopped out of luxury cars during morning drop-off and whose private tutors regularly visited their sprawling, river-front homes to ensure they made As in all their classes. Their world wasn't my world, but I still measured myself against the rubric of their GPAs and lifestyles. And I felt I was lacking in every way. The more I compared myself with them, the less sure I was about why I was there.

———— ⨯⨯⨯ ————

Success is a subjective word. For some people, success is having a job that covers the bills and leaves a little extra money to take in a movie occasionally. For other people, success is only success if there is more money in the bank than they could ever possibly need. Some people think success is being able to look around a dinner table and see the familiar, smiling faces of family and friends. Yet other people measure success by the number of awards lining the mantel of their fireplace. Success is truly in the eye of the beholder, and as such, success is vulnerable to being defined by proxy, using one thing as a measure for something else. In many of our cases, we mistakenly use other people's achievements, or lack thereof, as the proxy for our own value.

Comparison is dangerous because it requires the use of false equivalence. False equivalence happens when we compare two things to each other that are fundamentally different and therefore can't be compared, such as apples and oranges. If we put an apple and an orange on trial to find out which is better, the only thing they have in common enough to compare is their shape. And because of that, there is no way to compare them and determine which is "better."

Yet this is often how we approach our understanding of our value as individuals. You look around at the oranges, pears, and bananas of other people's lives to determine how valuable your apple is when there is no external comparison for the intrinsic worth God embedded in you before you were a seed in your mother's womb. In Jeremiah 1:5 God assured Jeremiah, "Before I formed you in the womb I knew you, before you were born I set you apart; I appointed you as a prophet to the nations." Many people know this verse, but the verse that follows contains Jeremiah's response: "'Alas, Sovereign LORD,' I said, 'I do not know how to speak; I am too young.'" In other words, Jeremiah felt inadequate because he looked around at the other prophets who were older and compared his age with theirs.

As much as I appreciate the role social media plays in connecting me with the people I find interesting, I've had to stop following some people because the things they share from their lives leave me feeling bad about my own *by comparison.*

I have a *great* life, but when they post images from their latest two-week exotic vacation filled with blissful massages and rest upon rest, while I'm falling into bed exhausted and peeling myself out of bed the next day *still* exhausted, my life suddenly feels inadequate. When they post their latest luxury handbag that I *know* retails for more than $10,000 because I politely put it back on the shelf when I was at the boutique and found out how much it cost, my income suddenly feels inadequate. When they post the latest celebrity-stylist-designed custom ensemble that they wore to another weekly exclusive event that I didn't even know existed, I suddenly feel inadequate as a person. Watching more and more of the perfectly curated lives some people present to the world left me less satisfied with my own. So I did the best thing for me; I clicked "unfollow" on every account that left me feeling as if my life wasn't enough. That *I* wasn't enough.

> You are the only you who ever has been and ever will be.

We all face the daily danger of defining ourselves based on what others achieve, but a powerful mantra most athletes observe is "*You* are your only competition." Think about it. No matter how fast another person may run their race, you will only run as fast as *you* can. And this is why the only goal you can ever achieve is the goal of beating your own records. When God created you, he literally broke the mold. There is no other you. Nowhere on earth. Not today. Not yesterday. Not ten years from now. You are the only you who ever has been and ever will be, so what a shame it would be for you to be born as *you* but to live your entire life trying to be someone else, someone you could never be no matter how hard you try, anyway. There is no one else on this earth whom you can compare yourself with because, like apples and oranges, you have only one characteristic in common with that other person—your humanity. We are all fallible human beings. No matter how many followers they have on social media or how much money they have in their bank or how many people know their name, they still have to sit on a toilet as you and I do throughout the day, although their toilet may be 24K gold, self-cleaning, and automatically spray Chanel No. 5 after they flush. Same difference.

Comparing yourself to others is like comparing a Van Gogh to a da Vinci. They're both priceless works of art, but that's where the similarities end. There is no way to establish the worth of one by looking at the other. The only way to establish the value of each piece is to evaluate them individually for their unique attributes. No art dealer worth their salt would say, "Well, comparatively speaking, the way da Vinci treated the materials in this work makes it less valuable because of the way Van Gogh treated the materials in that work." Each work of art is uniquely valued on its own accord. Just as you are.

You are a work of art, crafted by the greatest artist in the history of the universe. He created time, the heavens, the earth, every kingdom, genus, and species known and unknown to humanity. And he created you. Uniquely. You are a one-of-a-kind priceless treasure, but past pain can deceive you into basing your worth on the perceived value of another work of art that's scrolling by in your Instagram feed or working across from your cubicle. Since there isn't anyone else on this earth like you, comparing yourself with other people is like comparing the north to the south or the east to the west. They each serve a directional purpose, but none is "better" than the others. No one would say, "If I had my choice, I would only drive south" or "I gotta be honest, I'm more of an eastern-facing kind of girl." Silly, right? But that's what we do when we shift our focus away from the unique gifts, calling, and purpose God has given us and instead focus on the gifts, calling, and purpose in other people's lives.

Your only competition is the person staring back at you in the mirror every day. In the world of running, the abbreviation *PR* stands for personal record and is used to describe the victory of running faster than *you* ever have before. Only one person is ahead of you in the race of life— the person God created you to be. Catching up requires no longer looking around to see what others are doing. It's just you versus you. And personal progress is about making sure you win every time.

∞∞∞

Thomas Jakes spent his teen years caring for his ailing father while working in the local industries in South Charleston, West Virginia. He felt a call to the ministry, so he enrolled in classes at West Virginia State University but soon dropped out. He took a job at a local factory and started preaching around town occasionally. He married in the summer of 1982 and that same year was invited to pastor a small church with only ten members. The church was in disrepair and he made little money, but he set aside what he could from his factory salary to fix it up. The church grew over the next few years, but despite the growth, he still couldn't afford to buy the nice suits and shoes other pastors wore. He had so little money that he often wore the same suit everywhere he went, a practice that earned him the nickname "One-suit Jakes."

Although he smiled at the jokes, they hurt him deeply. He had big dreams and an incredible gift for preaching, but the voices in his life and mind spoke against what he felt in his heart. He tried to laugh off people's mean-spirited comments, but they pierced his soul in a deeply painful way, making him wonder, "Am I really meant to do this?" From everything he could see, success looked as though it eluded him, *when compared with others*. But one day, in complete discouragement and defeat, he determined to never again allow others to distract him from what he knew God had placed inside him.

He completed a bachelor's degree and master's degree in 1990, then in 1995, he completed a doctor of ministry in religious studies, changing his title from Pastor Thomas Jakes to Dr. Thomas Jakes. In May 1996 the "one-suit preacher," who had endured the ridicule and jokes of so many, moved his family and fifty other families from his church in West Virginia to Dallas, Texas, where he purchased a church building and renamed it The Potter's House. The man now known around the world as Bishop T. D. Jakes went from serving a ten-member church with holes in the roof in 1982 to thirty years later leading a congregation of thirty thousand people, with a global ministry that touches the far corners of the earth.

Of his journey, Bishop Jakes said, "The acorn contains the entire oak tree, but you can't see the future oak tree from looking at the present acorn. I had to learn to value the acorn that was inside me, even when other oak trees laughed at me. That which we are to become is already within us. We just don't see it yet."[1]

Rising from the pain that lies *behind* us requires focusing on the purpose that lies *within* us. Think about all the people in your life whom you compare yourself with: that sibling who got married first, despite being younger; that coworker who always comes into the office looking flawless when you're just trying not to show up with your baby's spit-up on your shirt; that college roommate who was just elected to the office of governor when *you* were the student body president but now process pay-roll for a doctor's office. Write their names down on a piece of paper along with a narrative about the part of your identity

> Rising from the pain that lies *behind* us requires focusing on the purpose that lies *within* us.

that you have been comparing to them and why. Then out loud, one by one, surrender your insecurities to God, and ask God to help you focus on yourself in order to discover the truth that you are enough.

In the case of the younger sibling who got married while you remain single, this could look like the following:

> Lord, I love my sister. And I want the best for her. But seeing her happy and building a life with her husband makes me feel as though something is wrong with me. It feels as if everyone else believes something is wrong with me too, because they keep asking me when I'm getting married, as if it's my decision. Father, help me to release myself from the expectations that have created the disappointment I'm battling with. Help me enjoy watching my sister's happiness as much as I would enjoy sharing in it. I accept that I am enough as I am. May your grace cover my desires so that I can focus on the purpose and plan you have for me. Amen.

This process isn't a one-and-done scenario. You will need to seek God daily for freedom from comparison. With every post we see on social media, with every awards show on television, with every feature story on the cover of your favorite magazine, there is going to be the temptation to view your life in comparison with the lives of others. But as you begin to intentionally untether your sense of personal worth from what others' lives look like, you will discover the fulfillment of fully occupying the unique purpose God has placed in you. You will come to realize that no matter how successful you may have thought you were in comparison to others, there is nothing like the "good" success found in God.

Chapter 7

Success versus *Good* Success

"You should run," said my tenth-grade public speaking teacher. "You have such a great presence and speak with such conviction. I think they would vote for you."

I was contemplating running for sophomore class president and asked Ms. Penny for her opinion. She couldn't have been more enthusiastic. I loved all my classes, but her public speaking class was the one I couldn't wait to get to every day. My classmates dreaded Fridays—speech days. Most of them stood at the podium in the front of the class and stared down at the index cards they were gripping for dear life while reading the words they had written as if they were someone else's. Me? I started memorizing my speeches. Having to shuffle index cards or flip papers felt like a distraction from the ideas I wanted to communicate, so I memorized enough of my content to focus on how I expressed it instead of what I was expressing.

The first time I presented from memory, Ms. Penny asked me to stay after class and said, "Nona, you have a gift. I've been doing this a long time, and I've never found myself so enraptured in a student's speech. I looked around the room, and everyone was just as engaged as I was. That's real, raw talent. I can't teach you how to do what you naturally do, but I can help you do it better, if you let me."

When Fridays came around, I couldn't wait to stand at that podium to deliver the week's topic and get Ms. Penny's critique to make me better the following week. And when I decided to run for sophomore class president, it was Ms. Penny who heard my speech the evening before election day and helped me refine my points and my delivery. When the time came to deliver my election-day speech to my 864 classmates gathered in the main auditorium, I looked out across their clearly bored faces and calmly, confidently expressed why I was best suited to lead them.

In my concluding line, I announced, "Yesterday is history. Tomorrow is still a mystery. But today is God's gift. That's why it's called the present. With me as your sophomore class president, we will open the gift of the present together and build a future we can all be proud of."

My classmates erupted in applause and elected me by a landslide.

As class president, I was suddenly ushered into a realm of student life that included regular meetings with the principal, deans, and department chairs. By virtue of my position, I was selected to represent the school at statewide and national student leadership conferences, and I was given speaking roles at schoolwide events such as pep rallies and spirit days. Although the term *influencer* wasn't a thing then, I was definitely a young influencer at my school, if ever there was one. People in grades ahead of me knew my name, and I was viewed as a "star student" by teachers and administrators alike because, in addition to my leadership role in student government, I had a

4.0 GPA across all honors classes. I was considered a success by every measure possible for a tenth-grader and had honed a lively, bubbly, approachable personality that afforded me a cadre of friends at all grade levels, but at the core of my being, a dangerous shift was happening. Whereas being labeled a "problem child" in elementary school made me live down to people's expectations, getting labeled a "star student" in high school made me base my value on other people's high expectations. And despite what it looked like on the outside, I was deeply insecure.

Many of us are living our lives through the expectations of others. Maybe people say you're smart, so you study hard to prove them right. People say you're lazy, so you don't even try to prove them wrong. People say you're argumentative, so you hold your tongue until you blow up and everything spews freely from your heart. Or people say you're nothing special, and you begin to believe them.

I modulated my behavior in middle school on the basis of the external validation of my teachers, but the root of that change wasn't a personal desire to be better; it was the insecurity of wanting, needing, attention. More than anything, I just wanted attention. I wanted someone to notice me. I wanted to be worthy of the time it took to acknowledge that I existed. So when I got attention in elementary school by acting out, that's what I continued to do, and when I started getting attention for achieving good grades in middle school, I shifted my focus there. Who I was never changed. I simply changed the way I *expressed* myself. Maybe you have done the same.

Depending on whom you ask, people may have varying experiences with you. Some would say you're a generous person, but others would say they've known you to be selfish. Your boss thinks your coworker is the greatest gift to the company, while you and your colleagues watch them cut corners on a regular basis. This emotional, psychological, and mental shape-shifting takes a toll not only on others but also on you. When you aren't certain of your unique identity in the world, it's difficult to be certain of your purpose in the world. And when you aren't certain of your purpose in the world, you might achieve success, but it won't be success *on purpose*. People may think you're the greatest thing since avocado toast, but in the absence of purpose, success will leave a lingering emptiness inside. And that emptiness will drive you to pursue more achievement, only to find more emptiness on the other side of the money, fame, and awards.

> What people think *about* you is your reputation, but who you *are* on the inside is your character.

What people think *about* you is your reputation, but who you *are* on the inside is your character. If our character isn't rooted in who God says we are and what God has called us to do, we will do anything for anyone who offers applause in our direction.

After being promoted to advanced classes in sixth grade, I changed my approach to school entirely. I became studious and outgoing, behavior that rewarded me with privileges instead of the punishment I was used to in elementary school. One day I saw a flyer advertising tryouts for our middle school dance team and decided to do it. When I arrived at the tryouts, the gym was filled with girls dressed in strange clothes—weird tights, shorts with slits up the side, and flowing tops. I wore my gym clothes, a pair of old shorts, and an old shirt. I didn't know at the time that there was such a thing as "dance clothes" or "dance classes," but I learned from one of the girls sitting near me as we waited to start that she had been "in dance" since she was two. Other girls shared similar experiences, some discussing ballet and modern dance as their favorites. The only things I knew about dance were the "running man," the "cabbage patch," and the "typewriter."

"All right, ladies! Line up. I'm going to teach you a routine, then you're going to be placed in groups to perform it. Let's go," shouted a tall, beautiful black woman I had never seen before.

She pressed play on a CD player and counted as she danced, "One, two, three, four, five, six, seven, eight." As she danced, the girls around me mimicked her movements. I wasn't sure why they did that since I thought we were coming to show our dance moves, but I quickly picked up that we were expected to do what she did, so I paid attention. After showing the routine the fourth time, she counted us out into groups of five, then called each group one by one to perform the routine for her. When it was my group's turn, she pressed play and shouted out, "Five, six, seven, eight." My group began to move, and I realized I was supposed to join their movements, so I danced the moves I remembered her doing. When all the groups had gone, she had all the groups stand in front of her as she called out names from each group to advance to the next round of the tryout. Thankfully, my name was called. She repeated the process for the second round, teaching a different routine and evaluating our performance in different groups. My name was called again for the final round. In the final round, she taught the group a routine but made us perform it individually. When the round was finished, my name was called, and I was selected for the team.

I learned that the woman's name was Ms. Gilman when I saw her name on the permission form she passed around. The form congratulated us on being selected for the team, then outlined the expectations and costs for joining. It hadn't occurred to me that there would be a cost to join the team, and when I saw a joining fee of seventy-five dollars, I knew I would have a problem when I got home. Mom had started receiving a monthly social security check for me as partial replacement of Daddy's earnings after he died, but she always made me feel as though my existence was a financial burden to her. Anything that required her to spend money on me was a battle.

"Mom, I made the dance team at school," I said with a knot in my stomach.

"Okay," she said without looking away from the television.

"And you have to sign a form giving me permission to join the team . . . and . . . and . . . I have to pay a fee to join . . . and for uniforms."

"What? Pay how much?"

"Well, it's seventy-five dollars to join and—"

"Seventy-five dollars! Where are you going to get that kind of money? I don't work as hard as I do just to throw money away!"

"But, Mom, you're spending money on those parties every weekend! Can you just not have one?"

My mom looked at me as though she hoped I would die.

"How *dare* you question how I spend *my* money! It's *my* money!"

"Well, what about my social security check? You get money every month for me from Daddy dying."

"That's my money too! You ain't got no money in this house!"

"But—"

"But nothing. Get out of my face!"

I returned to my room feeling completely defeated. I had managed to make it through three rounds of auditions for the dance team, only to have my mom deny me the chance to join the team. I had never seen my social security check, but I heard her talk about it and knew it was several hundred dollars every month. When combined with Lee's disability check and the income from her job, I never knew her to struggle for money, which is why it always confused me when she found a way to blame me for money being "tight." There was always new furniture being delivered or new cars being purchased or weekend parties being thrown. With a broken heart, I prepared myself to tell Ms. Gilman the next day that I couldn't join the team and went to sleep. When I woke up and started getting ready for school, I saw a piece of paper on my dresser. It was a check for seventy-five dollars. I don't know what made my mom change her mind, but I was grateful and told her thank you before I left.

School, dance practice, and homework divided my days. Basketball season required us to dance at games every Thursday or Friday, and football season required us to dance at games every Friday or Saturday. My favorite games were away games because I got to see other schools and other parts of town. Most of my teammates' parents attended the games to cheer their daughter on during halftime, but I knew not to look in the stands for my mom. She had said early on, "I ain't got time for that," so I got rides back home after the games from other teammates' families. When tryouts came around again at the beginning of eighth grade, Ms. Gilman asked me and a few other girls to lead the tryouts as part of an audition for team captain. After auditions ended, she made me the captain of the dance team. I was floored. And honored.

Having never led anything before, being "in charge" provided me with a new sense of purpose. When people came to me for guidance, direction, or decision, I felt as though I mattered. Although subtle at the time, leading that team birthed a toxic desire that would later drive my decision to run for sophomore class president—the desire for importance. As captain, I was the one calling out the movements.

> A desire for the external affirmation of importance is often an outgrowth of internal feelings of insignificance.

I was the first person on the court or field. I was physically placed front and center of every routine so the other dancers could see me. And I loved it. But a desire for the external affirmation of importance is often an outgrowth of internal feelings of insignificance. It certainly was for me.

———— ∞ ————

Maybe you can relate. Maybe you pursued an opportunity, not because of what you could offer to *it* but because of what you thought it would say about *you*. You applied for that director job because you thought everyone would be impressed by your title. You placed your name on the ballot to run for city council because you wanted to hear "the honorable councilmember" whenever people said your name. You left the church where your pastor cared about you to start a new church because having people call *you* pastor made you feel special. But when you got that director's job, the team was a mess, and you crumbled under the pressure. You wanted the dream but not the dysfunction. When you got elected to the city council, every meeting was filled with controversy and hostility. You got called despicable instead of honorable. When you launched that new church, the three members who left your former pastor to join you ended up leaving and going back. You loved the platform but didn't love the people. Ambition has the power to attain success, but only character can make that success good.

When the children of Israel were taken into captivity in Egypt by Pharaoh, God raised up a leader in Moses to set them free. The children of Israel were granted freedom, but the journey to the new land God had promised them ended up taking forty years. It should have taken only eleven days. The people's hearts were full of ungratefulness, disobedience, and pride, so much so that God decided not to allow their generation to inherit the promised land but instead for their children to inherit it. After Moses died, God gave Joshua instructions on how to lead the children of Israel into the future, saying in Joshua 1:8, "This Book of the Law shall not depart from your mouth, but you shall meditate on it day and night, so that you may be careful to do according to all that is written in it. For then you will make your way prosperous, and then you will have good success" (ESV).

There is a lot to unpack in this one verse, beginning with God making a conditional promise of success to Joshua that rests on Joshua's knowledge of, adherence to, and application of God's Word in his life. Second, God's use of the qualifier "good" to describe success is quite interesting because success by definition is good. The opposite of success is failure, so why is God saying there is a higher level of success than *just* success? I believe the answer is found in his encouraging Joshua to build the type of character that would allow him to make his *own* way prosperous so that he would have good success.

By definition we succeed when we accomplish the aim we set out to accomplish. But what if our aim is off? What if we think we're aiming for a position, when in truth we're aiming for a sense of importance? And after we achieve that fancy title, the workload leaves us feeling stressed out and bitter because of all we had to go through to achieve and maintain the position. Have we *truly* succeeded? What if we think we're aiming for more followers on Instagram, when in truth we're aiming for a sense of self-worth? Even after achieving a large following, we still feel inadequate because someone else has more. Have we *truly* succeeded? What if we think we're aiming for a ten-thousand-member church, and after the eleven thousandth member, we still feel unfulfilled because other churches topped the list of the "fastest growing churches in America"? Have we *truly* succeeded?

I believe *good* success is measured only by the fruit of the success we achieve, so achieving an aim that ultimately leaves us feeling isolated, angry, hopeless, and overwhelmed may meet the definition of success, but it certainly isn't *good*. Have you ever found yourself in a situation where everyone was applauding you, but you secretly wished you could walk away from it all? I'm friends with a number of people who are considered successful from the outside looking in, but they have confided in me a deep desire to quit while at the top of their game. They grace the covers of magazines, are interviewed on prime-time television, deliver keynotes before gatherings of tens of thousands, then return to their five-star hotel room feeling empty and alone.

I've been there myself. What many would call success has had me flying first-class around the world, staying in exclusive resorts, buying expensive clothes, bags, and shoes, and eating the finest food. But the external expressions of success belied my internal feelings of failure, because I didn't have success; *success had me.* The expression "trappings of success" is appropriate because many of the wealthiest, most powerful people in the world feel trapped in their success. Past pain can fuel you to achieve great things, but it doesn't build the type of character that will allow you to enjoy the great things you achieve. Instead, past pain is a vacuum that never fills or satiates. The more you achieve, the more you need to achieve. It's been said that when a wealthy man was asked how much money was enough, he offered a one-word response: "More."

> Success doesn't change you; it reveals you.

How we pursue success says as much about us as how we act after we succeed, because success doesn't change you; it reveals you. And perhaps this has been you. You've been on a never-ending search for more, better, bigger, higher. But instead of relishing in the success you've attained, the only thing you consistently feel is a sense of lack. Perhaps past pain and insecurities have led you to jockey for positions and promotions and orchestrate your way into opportunities, but the work of it all has left you adrift with a question of purpose. It is at this important inflection point that God is calling to you and me, saying, "Be strong and very courageous, being careful to do according to all the law that Moses my servant commanded you. Do not turn from it to the right hand or to the left, that you may have good success wherever you go" (Joshua 1:7 ESV).

———— ∞∞∞ ————

It was 2005, and Donna was at the top of her game. She had just been named one of the seventy-five most powerful blacks in corporate America by *Black Enterprise* magazine. She was making millions of dollars every year leading a mortgage banking company and an international annuities and pensions operation for a Fortune 100 company out of Columbus, Ohio. She was a member of several corporate boards and exclusive organizations for the top executives in the world. But on January 21 of that year, she woke up feeling tired and groggy and struggled to walk to the bathroom. Her husband walked in to find her lying on the floor unable to move or talk, and he quickly called paramedics.

When she arrived at the emergency room, the team ran a battery of tests and diagnosed her with a transient ischemic attack, a ministroke, placing her at high risk for a full stroke. She was stunned. She wasn't overweight. She'd never had high blood pressure. Her cholesterol was always normal. And there hadn't been a history of stroke in her family. How could this have happened to an otherwise healthy forty-eight-year-old woman? That day was a wake-up call.

Until she landed in the hospital, Donna James had been a hard-charging, high-powered executive who had defied all odds for success. When she was just sixteen years old, she gave birth to a son, and she had to deal with not only the physical and economic challenge of being a teen mom but also an emotional challenge—shame. She was the last person her family would have expected to get pregnant. She was bright, ambitious, and clearly heading toward becoming the first person in her family to go to college. But their esteem of her great potential turned into the regret of great disappointment when she became pregnant. Her teachers started avoiding her, and her friends stopped speaking to her, causing Donna's shame to become deeply rooted in her heart, and she said, "It's an emotional burden of a magnitude I'm not even sure I can express. It's a shame spiral. It's a judgment spiral. Getting out of that spiral is the most important thing you can do."[1]

She became determined to succeed despite people's low expectations of her, and she did. She graduated from college and threw herself into the corporate world with an ambition fueled by a desire for redemption, and as she worked her way up the corporate ladder, she found herself in love with the challenge of each job. But she says, "The stress levels were high and the hours were long. I knew I was stressed, but I've always been stressed. It was what I considered normal stress. I felt like I was handling everything. Though I did spend most of my time on the job, it was a job I loved dearly. I loved the excitement, the challenge, the diversity."[2]

But after her ministroke, she reevaluated what was most important in her life and realized her body was speaking to her. Her health care team was unable to identify what caused the ministroke, but they agreed that the stress of the job most likely contributed to it. She retired from her career and shifted her focus to the personal passions that are deeply meaningful to her, such as helping pregnant and parenting teen moms.

The trauma of my past made me view titles as validation of my worth, and that struggle has continued throughout my life. But discovering the difference between success and *good* success has allowed me to feel worthy no matter where I sit on an organizational chart. Like Donna, you may have disappointed people in the past and are pursuing external success in hopes of rewriting the narrative they have about you in their minds. But I want to assure you that the only narrative that matters is the one in your heart. Even though you may have failed, you are *not* a failure. Even though you may have disappointed people, you are *not* a disappointment. Even though you *made* a mistake, you are *not* a mistake. When these thoughts cloud your mind and you start searching the horizon for the next thing to add to your resume, I want you to know that good success is not something you attain; good success is something you choose. God has said that good success happens when you do what he says, so it is up to you to choose to follow his blueprint for your life because when you do, "you will make your way prosperous, and then you will have good success" (Joshua 1:8 ESV).

> Good success is not something you attain; good success is something you choose.

Now we know surviving is not enough and have identified the enemy within. We've released ourselves from the why of our past and made the decision to choose freedom. We know we are never beyond repair and have determined to run our own race. Now that we understand the difference between success and good success, it's time to explore the blueprint for succeeding—a blueprint etched on purpose.

part 2

A BLUEPRINT FOR
SUCCESS

Success On Purpose

I've always loved science, especially the life sciences—biology, anatomy, physiology, biochemistry, and more. I took every science class offered in high school. I even took Physics I and Physics II as elective courses in place of recreation or art because I loved science so much. Science explained the "what" and "how" of the world to me, and the more I learned, the more I was in awe and wonder at the majesty of God. This is why the well-documented tension between the world of science and the world of faith has always perplexed me. While science does an incredible job of explaining the "what" and the "how" of life, only faith in God and his Word is capable of explaining the "why." *Purpose* is defined as "the reason for which something is done or created,"[1] and in the absence of that reason, the "what" and "how" become meaningless. A life lived apart from God is a life devoid of purpose because we can only understand why we were created by looking to our Creator.

> A life lived apart from God is a life devoid of purpose because we can only understand why we were created by looking to our Creator.

Adam and Eve were created as the perfect, incarnate reflections of God. In them resided the fullness of God's character, beauty, and identity. But when they lost fellowship with God and had to leave the garden of Eden, they didn't lose only *companionship* with God, they also lost the part of their *identity* that was fully satisfied in God. If you remember the story, it wasn't until after they ate the fruit of the forbidden tree that they suddenly realized they were naked. It wasn't until *after* they disobeyed God that they felt a need for clothing. Something was lost. Before that moment, simply being in the physical presence of God was enough. He provided a constant reminder of their purpose and reason for being because he was their Creator. But when that relationship was lost, a God-sized void filled their hearts, a void that has been passed down to all of us.

Many of us have been struggling to rise from our past because a void of purpose has left us feeling as if our only option to deal with our hurt is to grit our teeth and push through the pain. When the husband you gave the best years of your life to walks in early one morning and says, "I don't love you anymore. I'm leaving," where is purpose? When the child you sacrificed for to put through private school gets arrested for stealing something you would have bought them had they asked, where is meaning? When your manager spreads lies about you in hopes of limiting your advancement options so you'll stay on their team, where is reason?

In my case, it wasn't until I moved away to college and had the physical, emotional, and spiritual distance from my past that I was able to discern what God was building in me through the pain of my childhood. I have held high-level leadership roles for the last thirteen years of my career. I have started and led several entrepreneurial ventures and have spoken into the lives of countless individuals and professionals who are also battling through brokenness. Through those experiences, it is the clarity of hindsight that gives me the confidence to assure you that *good* success is built on the foundation of purpose. There is a reason for the pain, and once you understand your purpose, you will be able to build a fulfilling future.

> *Good* success is built on the foundation of purpose.

Good success, which brings peace, requires understanding the purpose of past pain. But understanding your purpose doesn't mean knowing why something happened in your past; understanding your purpose means knowing why it was necessary for your future. Success that emanates from the inside out sees the purpose for past pain as helping us build:

- <u>Gratitude</u>: All things work together for my good in the end.
- <u>Character</u>: What I do when no one's looking says more about me than my resume does.
- <u>Work ethic</u>: Every assignment I have is designed to showcase my reverence for God.
- <u>Curiosity</u>: I will never know it all, and therefore, being teachable is more valuable than being right.
- <u>Love for people</u>: The people in my life are more important than the task on my to-do list.
- <u>Righteousness</u>: I look to God and his Word for the answers to life's questions.

We will explore these principles one by one as played out in my life and the lives of others over the next several chapters because everything we've experienced in the past is being orchestrated by God for our future. And knowing this truth gives us a springboard from which we can begin to build gratitude. Let's get started.

Chapter 8

Build Gratitude

"You intended to harm me, but God intended it for good to accomplish what is now being done, the saving of many lives" (Genesis 50:20).

When Joseph made this statement, more than twenty years had gone by since his brothers had sold him into slavery. He had been rejected, imprisoned, starved, lied about, forgotten, and had lost all hope in the process. Yet as he sat on his throne as prime minister of Egypt that day, a role he wouldn't have been in had his brothers *not* sold him into slavery, Joseph realized that the harm he suffered in the past was used by God for his good and the good of others. Joseph was seventeen years old when he became an Egyptian slave, but now he was second in command to Pharaoh, the ruler of Egypt. And he was grateful.

Unlike Joseph, many of us look back over the hurtful things that happened to us, and instead of seeing the grace of God, we see a miscarriage of justice. The car accident that left you paralyzed. The coworker who lied about you to get your promotion. The boyfriend who promised he had been faithful, then had to admit he got another girl pregnant. That one happened to me. When we sit and stew in the pain of it all, we become blind to the grace God extends us in every moment of heartache. And we miss out on the gift of gratitude.

"And the winner is . . . Nona!"

"And the award goes to . . . Nona!"

"And in first place is . . . Nona!"

By the time I graduated from high school, I had accumulated so many awards, recognitions, and honors that the one and only college I applied to accepted my application early *and* offered me a full academic scholarship. I was heading to the University of Florida. For free. The once-reserved girl who was relegated to the corners of elementary school classrooms because of "bad behavior" was now a model student in the top 5 percent of her class, playing on the varsity tennis team, and was selected by a panel of her peers, teachers, and administrators to deliver the commencement address for her graduating class. Publicly, I had it all and my future was bright. But privately, I was battling the shadows of trauma while living in a dysfunctional home.

I had been introduced to a new church at the beginning of my junior year, thanks to a friend who invited me. I loved it the moment I walked in and ended up joining the same day. Soon after I joined, the pastor asked me to become a youth ministry leader. Later on, his wife encouraged me to join the choir after overhearing me singing from the audience. One night, when I thought no one was around, I started tinkering on the keyboard with the song we would be practicing that night. I had started playing the piano by ear in sixth grade but had never played for anyone publicly because I was embarrassed that I didn't know what I was doing. I didn't know the pastor's wife was standing in the back listening to me play. She was a musician herself and had sung professionally, so she walked up and said, "Why didn't you tell me you could play the keyboard? You're playing for us Sunday."

My heart dropped. I refused and quickly got up from the keyboard, pointing out that I didn't know how to play. She made me sit back down and play for her, then showed me how to play chord inversions to make the music sound richer.

That following Sunday, she directed the choir and periodically smiled over at me as I butchered my way through "I Will Bless the Lord" by Hezekiah Walker. After the music was fully massacred and the song ended, she ran over to me and gave me a tight hug and whispered, "I'm so proud of you." She continued to make me play each week. As I bumbled my way through more new music, she mentored me and honed my skill.

The summer before my senior year, I felt a call to preach. After sharing my feelings with the pastor, he agreed and scheduled me to deliver a trial sermon a few Sundays later. In many churches and denominations, a trial sermon is considered the final step to a licensure or ordination process, but at our church, the trial sermon was viewed as the first step in a lifelong process of training. The pastor wanted to see what was "in me" before preparing me for a life of preaching, and since I hadn't preached before, he was eager to put me to the test.

The church was packed that morning, and the audience

included my mom and Lee. It was their first time ever attending church with me. The pastor introduced me as "a young woman with great potential to impact the world for Christ," then told everyone he knew I was called to preach the moment he met me. After he handed me the mic, I offered preliminary acknowledgments according to the protocol of the church, then said, "I'm grateful to have my mom here today for this moment. This is her first visit with us."

When I finished preaching, the pastor handed me my certificate of licensure and reintroduced me to everyone as *Minister* Nona. I felt so blessed that I was able to take that formal step into ministry in order to begin my formal training.

As everyone filed out of church that day, my mom asked an usher to take a picture of me, her, and Lee on the steps. We had never taken a picture together before, so I assumed it meant a new, positive chapter had begun in our relationship. Instead, as we drove home that day, my mom proceeded to curse me out for not acknowledging her "better" from the pulpit. She said I embarrassed her when I called out that it was her first time there, and she also felt I said "more nice things" about the pastor and his wife than I did about her. She called me ungrateful, selfish, and other vulgar things between profanities. She said the church members were fake and judgmental and that she would never go back again. All the love that I witnessed people extend to her and Lee had been twisted in her mind as condescension. I was stunned.

I didn't know what I did that was so wrong to make her blow up at me. She wasn't taking me home from jail; she was taking me home from *church*, where I had just been licensed into the gospel ministry. Although I didn't say anything from the back seat, tears of anger fell from my eyes. I didn't drink, do drugs, or go to parties. I just went to school, church, and tennis practice. Yet there she was, calling me the worst names possible. Names that didn't match the truth of who I was and didn't speak to the future I was building. The bitterness and resentment I had kept buried within me all those years overtook me that day, and I promised myself that I would never, *ever* return home once I left for college.

As my senior year came to an end and graduation came into view, Mom blew up at me again and said she wasn't coming to watch me deliver the commencement address at graduation. I didn't even care. Her continued absence from my life coupled with her constant degradation of my character, on top of the excuses she had made for Lee throughout my childhood, had so deeply embittered me toward her that I had become numb to her. She did decide to attend at the last minute, but by the time she made that decision, our relationship was already shattered.

When I was in the midst of the pain she caused me, all I could see was how she was hurting me. But I later came to see in hindsight how the never-ending grace of God would end up using that pain to help me, and others, in the future. Just as he used Joseph.

———⚬⚬⚬———

The human side of us looks at past hurts and struggles and doesn't see any goodness in our pain; we see only *pain* in our pain. At least I did. But when Joseph reflected on his long journey from slave to prime minister, he was able to see the goodness of God in his situation. How is that possible? How was he able to make sense out of a seemingly nonsensical situation? How was he able to find purpose in seemingly purposeless circumstances?

When I left for college, I was outwardly successful, optimistic, and confident, but inwardly I was churning with bitterness, insecurities, and anger. I loved Jesus, but I rehearsed my past pain so often that I had no real joy or gratitude for the truly miraculous things God had done for me.

The only thing rehearsing my pain did was make me hypersensitive to criticism. I took even benign suggestions for improvement as indictments on my worth as a human being. I enrolled at the University of Florida as a microbiology and cell science major and will never forget how I felt the first time my inorganic chemistry professor critiqued a paper I turned in. I had stayed up late the night before to make sure my logic was sound and had triple-checked my formulas to make sure my answers were correct. But when I got the paper back, there was so much red ink on it that I thought he bled on my paper. For days I sulked around campus, feeling like a failure and impostor. Amazingly, I had gotten an A on the paper. But the commentary made me feel as though it were an F. As though *I* were an F. I heard my mom's voice in my mind saying I wasn't going to be anything, that I was lazy, that I was dumb. And the feedback made me bitter.

> What happens in our present is always filtered through our past.

With the gift of hindsight, I can see that his feedback was intended to help me. But in that moment, because I was sitting in the emotional prison of my personal trauma and feelings of inadequacy, his feedback didn't help me; it destroyed me. I've come to believe that nothing that happens to us in the present is about only the present. What happens in our present is always filtered through our past. Have you ever worn a pair of smudged glasses or sunglasses?

The first thing you try to do is *ignore* the smudges and keep looking straight, then you try to adjust the glasses and see *around* the smudges. But eventually, you realize there is only one solution. You take off the glasses and wipe the lenses to remove the smudges because only then can you see without distortion, obstruction, or distraction. Past pain smudges the lenses of life. And ultimately, we all have to make decisions about what we're going to do about it.

After receiving the paper my professor marked up, I sat in my dorm room and prayed to God through tears about how I felt like a failure and didn't think I belonged in college anymore. I ran through a litany of grievances from my past, and when I finally quieted enough to hear the voice of God, I heard the Lord say, "Nona, the reason you're hurt by your professor's comments isn't because of what he said. It's because of what you believe about yourself. You have strongholds in your mind that need to come down." The revelation struck a chord within me. I remembered hearing a quote attributed to Eleanor Roosevelt that said, "No one can make you feel inferior without your consent." Until that moment, I had been consenting to an identity that had been spoken over me throughout my life. Even though I was outwardly "successful" in middle school and high school, I had continued to see myself as not good enough. The feelings of not belonging in my middle school advanced classes never stopped just because I made good grades. Even when I was selected as a National Achievement Scholar from my SAT scores, I *still* felt like a failure. I *believed* I was a failure.

It occurred to me that I was now physically distant from the source of my pain, but I was still carrying that pain with me everywhere I went because the pain was no longer *outside* of me, it was now *inside* me.

Maybe you understand. Maybe it's been months, years, or decades since the trauma that scarred you, but the pain is there when you open your eyes in the morning, when you close your eyes at night, and often it's there in your dreams as you sleep. I have discovered that the power to break the hold past pain has on your life requires something more powerful than the pain itself; it requires the power to cultivate gratitude for your past. The Bible says in 2 Corinthians 10:4–5, "The weapons we fight with are not the weapons of the world. On the contrary, they have divine power to *demolish strongholds*. We demolish *arguments* and *every pretension* that sets itself up against the knowledge of God, and we take captive *every thought* to make it obedient to Christ" (emphasis mine).

The battle I was engaged in and the battle you are engaged in is in our minds. It's in the way we *think about* what happened to us and in what we *believe* about ourselves and our situation. Building a successful future requires cultivating gratitude for your past.

> Building a successful future requires cultivating gratitude for your past.

The apostle Paul tells us in Philippians 4:8, "Finally, brothers and sisters, whatever is true, whatever is noble, whatever is right, whatever is pure, whatever is lovely, whatever is admirable—if anything is excellent or praiseworthy—think about such things." This verse compels us to actively search for the good in every situation, a message that is particularly striking since Paul wrote these words from prison. And the prisons of his time weren't air-conditioned with three meals a day as we know them today. In Paul's time prisons were rancid, insect-filled, and disease-laden, with the smell of death and squalor baked together through the heat of day. Yet in the midst of his worst, Paul exhorted all of us to keep our minds focused on God's best.

When I reflected on all I had been through, I could see God's grace shaping my life every step of the way. Even though many of my elementary school teachers had said I was a "problem child," God opened the eyes of my middle school teachers to my potential and caused them to favor me. Even though I didn't grow up in a Christian home, the Lord found me and connected me with people who would inspire my faith walk at a young age. Even though my mom spoke words of discouragement into my life, the people at church spoke life, healing, and encouragement. He orchestrated a full scholarship to the only school I applied to, though others who were equally qualified had been denied admission. As I gave my attention to the goodness of God, the struggles and disappointments began to lose their power to influence my mind. Instead, I rejoiced in God and thanked him for the journey because what some may have meant for evil, God intended for good.

———— ✺ ————

It was 2015, and Sheryl Sandberg was one of the most recognized people in the world. She attained fame and fortune across a career that included such high-profile positions as chief of staff to Treasury Secretary Lawrence Summers and vice president of global online sales and operations at Google. But it was her role as chief operating officer of Facebook, the world's largest social network, that catapulted her to international prominence.

In 2012 Sheryl was named to *Time*'s annual list of the one hundred most influential people in the world, followed closely in 2013 by the release of her *New York Times* best-selling book *Lean In.* In her book Sheryl attributed a great deal of her success to her husband, Dave Goldberg, a man whom she said supported her every step of the way, both professionally and in raising their children. Colleagues, friends, and family unanimously described him as kind, compassionate, and unassuming.

And then, the unimaginable happened.

On May 1, 2015, while on vacation together with friends in Mexico, Dave left Sheryl to go work out in the resort gym and suffered a heart arrhythmia that led to a catastrophic accident. Sheryl found him lying on the gym floor unresponsive, and he passed away at the hospital shortly after arrival. He was forty-seven years old.

"The grief felt like a void, like it was sucking me in and pushing on me, pulling me in and I couldn't even see or breathe," Sheryl said. "People who have been through things like this told me it gets better. And I really didn't believe them." The pain, confusion, and trauma of Dave's sudden death left Sheryl feeling lost. And their children also. In her book *Option B*, chronicling her grief and subsequent lessons from the process, Sheryl said that when they arrived at Dave's funeral, their children "got out of the car and fell to the ground, unable to take another step. I lay on the grass, holding them as they wailed."[1]

At the deepest, darkest moments of her despair, she returned to Facebook in a haze, her confidence shaken and her emotions shattered. She noticed that friends didn't ask how she was doing, and she said, "I felt invisible, as if I were standing in front of them but they couldn't see me."[2] And it was at that place of feeling hopeless, helpless, and broken that she discovered a seed of gratitude that blossomed into a sense of hope.

"I realized that it could have been worse. What if Dave was driving with our children in the car when he had his arrhythmia? What if my entire family had been killed? The pain of his death was unimaginable, but the thought of losing everyone gave me perspective and a sense of gratitude in my grief. My husband is gone, but our children are here and he lives in each of them."[3] In the depths of her pain, realizing that the situation could have been worse gave her a sense of gratitude, even amid tremendous loss.

Pain is heavy. It creates a burden on our soul that we don't have the strength to lift in our own power. Rising from pain requires something more powerful than the weight of the pain. And a spirit of gratitude that *actively* seeks out the good in every painful experience gives you that power. The first time I told someone what had happened to me was by accident. I had noticed my dormmate suddenly acting strangely. She wouldn't leave our room and kept the curtains drawn so that it was dark in the middle of the day when I left. While falling asleep one night, I heard her sniffling in the dark, so I turned on my study light and asked her whether she was okay. The frailness of her "yeah" let me know she wasn't okay. I pulled back my covers and sat up on my bed.

"What's wrong, Laura?"

"Nothing. I'm okay," she said while facing the wall, with the comforter draped over her head.

"Listen, I'm not just here as your dormmate. I care about you as a person. I can hear you crying. Look, whatever it is, you can tell me. I promise I won't say anything to anyone."

"I . . . I was . . ." She sat up in her bed and stared down at her hands. Her eyes were puffy and swollen from crying. "I went to a house party with some friends the other night and met a guy that seemed pretty cool. He lived in the house and invited me back to his room. We started making out, and he pushed me down onto the bed. I told him to stop, but he didn't. He . . . he raped me." She said it with such pain that I cried too.

She continued, "I'd never had sex before. And it hurt so bad. I kept begging him to stop and saying no. He covered my mouth with his hands. I feel . . . dirty. I feel . . . like trash. I feel . . . I just have this pain in my chest. I don't know what to do."

I walked over and knelt next to her bed and grabbed her hand. She was an atheist, so I didn't pray for her at that moment since I knew she wouldn't be able to receive my prayer. Searching for the words to comfort her, I simply said, "I understand how you feel." Seeing the puzzled look on her face, I continued by sharing my own story and how I understood feeling dirty and like trash. I told her how I blamed myself every time it happened and that God had to show me it wasn't my fault, despite my mom telling me it was. I told her that the pain in her body would go away, but the pain she felt in her heart, her soul, would need the type of healing that only God could provide. That night in our dorm, we read the Bible together and talked about Jesus. This was the same person who when I first moved in and she saw my Bible on my desk said, "Oh no. I hope you're not one of those Jesus freaks." Suddenly, she and I were knit together by shared trauma, but now I was in a position to lead her to faith in Christ to heal her from her pain.

While I wish I could have shared my story under

different circumstances, I learned an important truth that day: there is no way out of pain except *through* it. As I shared my story with her, it forced me to revisit the pain I had worked so hard to ignore. Yet as I spoke the words that had been buried deep within my heart, a remarkable thing happened. I realized that, like Joseph's pain, my pain could be used on purpose for the good of someone else. I've come to realize that we have to go *through* our dark places before we can emerge on the other side of them. And by walking through the pain, we can confront it and release the power that pain wields over our past.

> When we see the goodness of God in our past, we are able to build a strong foundation for our future.

Seeing my pain have the power to bring hope to someone made me grateful. And it's the reason I share my story so freely today. The trauma, desperation, isolation, and rejection I suffered has given birth to a story of faith, hope, love, and redemption that not only encouraged my college friend but has been an encouragement to thousands of people who have never given voice to their past. When we see the goodness of God in our past, we are able to build a strong foundation for our future. This is especially true when we allow God to use our past to encourage someone else.

Maybe you overheard your coworker crying in a bathroom stall and learned that her husband gave her divorce papers that morning. You walked that same path several years ago, and although it still hurts, you can let her know from experience that there is hope. You can point to your ex-husband's many affairs during your marriage that hurt worse than the divorce, and you can offer a shoulder to cry on. Or maybe your son hung up the phone and said, "I didn't get the job," through clenched teeth, trying to hold back tears. You can reflect on the time you also badly wanted a job but got passed over for it. You're able to tell him how that rejection was used by God to get you where you are now, and your encouragement can be based on your own lived truth that "all things work together for our good." By sharing your pain to comfort someone else, you can become grateful for the journey and what you've learned.

As you think about your past, in what ways can you see God orchestrating good through your pain? How do you think you can use your pain as a source of hope and wisdom for others? What do you need to be thinking on now that you know your battle is not with the people who hurt you but is instead with the thoughts that keep you meditating on the pain? Your pain is not your story; your pain is the prologue to your purpose.

> Your pain is the prologue to your purpose.

Discovering the good in your past will help you see the possibilities for your future. And as you build toward your future, a posture of gratitude will help you build the type of character you will need to sustain success for the long term.

Chapter 9

Build Character

"Look, this isn't working for me. I think we just need to go our separate ways."

It was my third year of college, and Tim, my boyfriend of six months, had called to break up with me. His words didn't sadden me. I was angry. The reason he gave for the breakup was that I was argumentative, an interesting rationale since my arguments were made only in response to his own.

"Cool, bye," I said, anger making my hands tremble as I hung up the phone.

I wasn't the type of person who created arguments for no reason, but I *was* the type of person who didn't run from an argument either. Having grown up in an environment where I had to silently suffer through my mom's constant tirades, I vowed never to allow anyone to silence my voice again, and when it came to Tim, he wouldn't only share an opinion, he would issue a decree from on high. Whether it was a matter of politics or career or faith or music, Tim would state his perspective as if it were canonized in Scripture. And I often didn't agree with him. So I told him he was wrong. Often.

He would make a declaration, and we would spend the next thirty to forty-five minutes offering point-counterpoint-point-counterpoint until, finally, one of us threw up our hands and said, "Forget it." Arguing was common to me because I grew up that way. Tim, on the other hand, saw the mental sparring matches as a sign of future trouble. And he was right. I was a regular on the dean's list and was chapter president of my sorority at the time, but despite the outward indicators of success, I had some character flaws that needed to be fixed.

Just as I had with the professor's comments on my paper, I saw Tim's disagreement with me as an indictment of my value as a human being. I had difficulty with criticism from an early age because I got so

> When we feel the need to defend ourselves, it means we feel there is something to lose.

much of it that I became defensive whenever I perceived that someone was coming against me. I didn't know how not to take it personally. When I argued with Tim, I wasn't fighting only to prove I was *right*, I was fighting to prove I was *worthy*. I was always trying to outrun the whispers of "you're not good enough." When he broke up with me, the pain of rejection became the catalyst that forced me to confront my feelings of unworthiness. Even though I was physically gone from the home where I had been violated, there were parts of me that still felt as though I needed to be defended. And when we feel the need to defend ourselves, it means we feel there is something to lose. But what was at stake for me?

Every one of us has an ideal depiction of ourselves—the self we want others to know. This public identity we work to curate is known as our reputation. We form our reputation by *behaving* in ways that we hope will make people see us the way we want to be seen.

In the first few months of our relationship, Tim thought I was an agreeable, mild-mannered woman who gladly went along with whatever he wanted to do, without complaint. I behaved that way in the beginning because that's exactly what I wanted him to believe about me. I wanted the relationship to work, so even when I didn't agree with something, I let it go for the sake of peace. Maybe you've done that before. You molded your behavior around the image you wanted to project, out of fear of losing the relationship. Maybe you got all dressed up for a date, but moments before you were set to leave, they texted to say they couldn't make it. Although you were furious and felt an explanation was deserved, you simply replied with, "Okay. Maybe next time (smiley face emoji)." Or maybe you made a new friend on the job, and when they started talking politics one day, you realized you're on opposite ends of the spectrum. But instead of saying anything, you simply nodded, smiled, and said, "I hear you." In both cases, you modulated your behavior in an effort not to "rock the boat" of your relationship. But your behavior didn't change your beliefs; it simply *belied* them.

> Your behavior didn't change your beliefs; it simply *belied* them.

While the way we behave creates our reputation, our behavior is an extension of our character. Proverbs 23:7 says, "As he thinks in his heart, so *is* he" (NKJV). It's what we believe that determines our character, and it's our character that drives our behavior. My initial attempts to change the way I came across to Tim were doomed from the beginning because in my heart I believed I was the only one who would ever protect me, so I needed to fight when challenged. By the time I grew weary of his pronouncements of opinion masquerading as fact, he had grown accustomed to my acquiescence and was taken aback the day I said, "Well, I disagree." The person he *thought* I was and the person I *really* was were not the same. My main stage persona was exactly what he wanted, but when the costume came off, he was confused. And that's why he broke it off. My reputation and my character weren't aligned because the successful person I was on the outside was the facade hiding who I was on the inside—a person who was deeply broken and damaged.

Have you ever wanted someone to like you, love you, choose you so badly that you hid the parts of you that you were afraid would make them run for the hills? You even accepted *their* bad behavior because you felt a sense of validation by having them in your life. Maybe you didn't make any demands on the relationship for fear of their walking away from you, and you ended up emotionally depleted, wearing a fake smile to cover the emptiness you felt. I've been there.

I walked with someone I considered a friend through a very difficult time in his life, but when it came time for him to return the favor and be the emotional ladder I needed to climb out of my own painful situation, he didn't have the time. The *one* day I called him to talk through a painful meeting with my mother in which she blamed me for what happened when I was a child, he rushed me off the phone. I had no one else to call and thought he was safe for me, but no.

But even after that experience, I was so broken that I continued to be there for him when he reached out. I accepted behavior from him that I know he wouldn't have accepted from me. Thoughts of inadequacy kept assuring me that it was enough for us to talk when he needed me, despite his absence when I needed him. And those wrong thoughts built a character in me that was both too passive and too defensive at the same time. I desperately wanted him to like me, but I also felt unworthy and unsure. The more I put his needs before my own, the less he respected me, and the more I sacrificed my character on the altar of needing to be needed. This is why God doesn't want to change our behavior; God wants to change our character. Our charac-

> God doesn't want to change our behavior; God wants to change our character.

ter is our identity—who we are when no one is looking. And God wants our character to be rooted in who *he* says we are.

For many of us, myself included, our sense of self-worth rises and falls with the opinions of other people. This is why, despite knowing how much God loved me and how special I was to him, I still felt the need to pursue achievement in school and in my career as a measuring stick of my value. Yet no matter how much I achieved and no matter how high my name rose on organizational charts, I still felt a nagging sense of unfulfillment. Sure, the excitement of a promotion or accolade would make me *happy*, but happiness is temporary because it lives in the realm of memories, which fade over time. The sense of unfulfillment we experience is a derivative of entangling our identity with the fleeting euphoria of temporal achievement. That's why good success has nothing to do with what we *achieve* for ourselves and everything to do with what we *believe* about ourselves.

We tend to base our beliefs about ourselves on what *others* say about us, but have you ever taken a moment to consider what *God* says about you? Although you may be surrounded by people or situations that remind you of your past, **you are *not* your past**: Romans 6:6, "We know that our old self was crucified with him so that the body ruled by sin might be done away with, that we should no longer be slaves to sin." Although you may have been told you were an unplanned pregnancy, **you have purpose**: Jeremiah 1:5, "Before I formed you in the womb I knew you, before you were born I set you apart; I appointed you as a prophet to the nations." Although you may feel as if nothing has worked out in your life the way you planned, **you are chosen**: 1 Peter 2:9, "You are a chosen people, a royal priesthood, a holy nation, God's special possession, that you may declare the praises of him who called you out of darkness into his wonderful light." Although you may look around at others and wish you could sing as they do or speak as they do or lead as they do, **you are gifted**: 1 Corinthians 12:4, "There are different kinds of gifts, but the same Spirit distributes them." Although you may be single (or married and feeling single), **you are loved**: John 3:16, "God so loved the world that he gave his one and only Son, that whoever believes in him shall not perish but have eternal life." And the one I needed to know the most—although you may have been told you aren't good enough or pretty enough or rich enough or smart enough, **you are worthy**: Romans 5:8, "God demonstrates his own love for us in this: While we were still sinners, Christ died for us."

As you meditate on who *God* says you are, you will no longer make choices based on the shifting needs and expectations of other people. I discovered that the more I understood my identity in Christ, the easier it was to believe what he said about me. And in believing what he said about me, my character stopped being driven by inadequacy and was finally replaced by the assurance that I was enough. In Christ.

He was married to literally the most beautiful woman in the world. His wife, Halle Berry, had been given that distinction by countless magazines. The day she won her Academy Award, Eric Benét was caught on camera gazing up at her as she accepted her award, with tears of pride in his eyes. Their fans were already smitten by their relationship, but seeing the genuine love he had for her on full display made hearts around the world swoon with joy and envy. Many women secretly hoped to find their own version of Eric Benét—a man who would love them, care for them, and support them as Eric did with Halle Berry. But just ten days after receiving that award, their lives changed forever.

Star magazine published a story that said Eric was cheating on Halle. Halle didn't even ask him whether it was true; she simply reached out to her lawyers to fight the salacious, scandalous, slanderous fabrication about her husband. She knew her husband to be faithful, loving, and kind and determined to lock arms with him in taking down the entire media enterprise. But as she got deeper into lawsuit mode, Eric told her the unthinkable. "It's true," he said. "I had an affair." Unfortunately, that revelation was just the beginning.

She was in London filming a movie when he flew to meet her to talk. It was there he recounted the many, many, many women he had been with throughout their relationship, and suddenly, Halle realized that the man she thought she knew so well was a complete stranger. "I had a perfect marriage. He was one of the kindest men I've ever known on many levels.

It was heartbreaking, and I couldn't understand why. I was devastated."[1] She was heartbroken, but purposed to find a way to fix it, even going so far as blaming herself for working too much. But she finally realized that something deep in him was broken, and she didn't have the power to fix it.

Eric brought issues and insecurities into the marriage, but the pressure of living up to a public reputation made it difficult to work on his private character issues. "Marriage is a challenge in itself," Eric said, "but when you have a marriage in a fishbowl that's onstage for the whole world to see—it's really hard to adjust to that." After the revelations about the affairs, he said, "I did a lot of therapy. I really felt like I had to find God. And he really needed to find me. God helped me to dig deep."[2]

Although their marriage didn't survive the revelations, Eric has reportedly done the heavy lifting he needed to do to reshape his character into one undefined by the need for women's attention. Instead, he sees his greatest accomplishment as raising his daughter to be the type of woman who knows what to expect from a good man— honesty, faithfulness, and fidelity, character qualities he has built from the ashes of his past failures.

Shortly after the breakup with Tim, I looked up to the ceiling of my apartment and said, "God, if you never allow me to get married, I will still choose you. You are the one I need because you know every part of me. I will serve you, even when what I want is not your will." A few weeks after that prayer, Tim called me out of the blue and asked me to join him and his family for dinner. We hadn't spoken much since the breakup, and although he jokingly said he figured I was waiting by the phone for his call, the truth was that I had moved on. Rejecting me was the best thing he could have ever done for me because it issued a wake-up call.

After changing my behavior to win his heart when we were together, only to eventually have him leave me once my true self came out, I recognized the need for an identity anchor. I spent my time studying God's Word and building my character to repair the parts of me that were still broken. I realized during our time apart that I had a deep need to matter to people, and although that is ingrained in all of us, the trauma of my childhood made it worse. When I got to a place that my full sufficiency was in God, I was glad to have Tim in my life, but I realized I could be just fine without him. And it wasn't until I believed that in my heart that I was ready for a relationship again.

I mentioned earlier that we feel the need to defend ourselves when we feel there's something to lose, and I discovered during my time of prayer that the stakes were so high because I had tied my identity to being wanted. My character was born out of feelings of inadequacy, and my actions toward Tim were driven from that place of pain. Maybe you can relate. Maybe the things you've believed about yourself have led you to take actions you regret. Maybe you've had a series of one-night stands with men you barely know because you believe you're damaged goods and nobody would ever want you. Maybe you stole money from the petty-cash drawer at your job because you believe you'll never get a promotion.

In either case, what you believed about yourself created the character that enabled the action, but at the root of the character that created the action was a basic belief that you have to prove you're worthy of people's time or attention. But if you base your decisions on what will make people like you, you will often find yourself in situations you never intended. Our identity should be rooted in who God says we are in his Word. And whether we get married or get that promotion doesn't change what God's Word says about us. Broken character isn't repaired by new *behavior*; it's repaired by new *beliefs*. And those new beliefs will lead to new behavior.

> Broken character isn't repaired by new *behavior*; it's repaired by new *beliefs*.

A couple of months after we rekindled our relationship, Tim asked me to marry him. The work God did in me had changed my beliefs about myself, and once my beliefs were changed, my behavior followed. I wasn't perfect and still struggle with criticism to this day, but my identity is anchored in God's Word, so I *grow* through every test, in pursuit of who he has called me to be. As we pursue success in its various forms, set your heart on attaining character more than a position, relationship, or wealth. Because in attaining character, you will show God that he can trust you to take care of whatever gifts he blesses you with down the line. In the absence of character, we will derive our value from things it was never intended to come from. And that's *everything* except God.

When we build character anchored in our identity in Christ, God will be able to trust us with his best gifts. And once God can trust you with his best gifts, your work ethic will be able to take you places where your character will allow you to *stay*.

Chapter 10

Build Work Ethic

Tim and I got married a month after I graduated from college, and we immediately moved into our first home together. I settled into life with my new husband and into a new job as a quality analyst for a large property and casualty insurance company. It was a far stretch from my initial plans of becoming a physician because, halfway through college, a bad experience during a summer medical research project made me change my plans. My project sponsor was a physician of more than thirty years who asked me one day why I wanted to become a doctor.

I looked up at him with big optimism-filled eyes and said, "I want to give people hope. I want to assure people that they have an advocate in me. I want to change the world one patient at a time."

As the violins I heard in my mind hit their crescendo, he simply rolled his eyes and said, "That's not what we do. Physicians are about medicine, science, and data. We're not here to give hope. We're here to do a job."

And with that inspiring encouragement, I decided medicine wasn't for me.

Shortly afterward, I changed my major from microbiology and cell science to telecommunications. I learned a few weeks into my new major that the College of Journalism produced the news for the local public broadcasting station and was holding auditions for anchors, so I gave it a shot and was selected. I loved the news and was good at it. I even landed a part-time, paying job in the "real world" as news director for the local radio conglomerate. I delivered the news during the *Tom Joyner Morning Show* and envisioned myself as a media maven like Oprah Winfrey someday. I was going to do radio, host a television show, and launch a magazine. But as graduation approached and the realities of the low pay, long hours, and cutthroat competition in the media industry sank in, I decided to look for something more traditional and found it at Nationwide.

I applied for a quality assurance analyst role, a job I wasn't qualified for. It required six years of management experience, but the job description sounded interesting, and the salary range was comfortable, so I figured I didn't have anything to lose by tossing my hat into the ring. I was surprised when I was asked to come in for an interview. Since I was fresh out of college without the requisite management experience, I figured I could at least look like a manager, so I went to J. C. Penney and bought the most manager-looking pantsuit possible. It was chocolate brown with large chocolate-brown buttons. I had pledged Alpha Kappa Alpha sorority in college and wore pearls almost daily as our signature jewelry, so I simply bought a new multistrand pearl necklace to complement the suit. When the day of the interview came, I put on my "manager costume" and made my way to the building for my interview.

After waiting in the lobby for a few brief minutes, a

woman in jeans and a T-shirt peered through the doorway and waved me in.

"Hey, Nona. My name is Tawney. I work in claims services."

"Oh, great! Hi, Tawney. Thanks for having me." I had always believed that no matter what someone looks like, you should treat them respectfully, so I gave her as much respect as I would give the hiring manager.

"Is this your first time here?" she asked while we walked up the stairs together.

"Oh, no. I worked part-time in the call center for a little while in college."

"I got my start in the call center," she said and added with a chuckle, "I think everyone starts in the call center!"

As we came to the top of the stairs, she led me into a small conference room and told me, "Sharon will be right in."

About five minutes later, Tawney walked back in with a notepad and pen, along with two other women. One of the ladies had on jeans and a T-shirt, and the other had on a suit quite like the one I was wearing. I figured she was Sharon.

"Hi, Nona! Sharon Tindley," she said with a light southern drawl and a smile. "This is my assistant, Amanda."

"Hi, Nona," Amanda said, extending her arm for a handshake.

"So nice to meet you all. Thanks for having me."

"Shall we get started?" Sharon asked.

For the next forty-five minutes, Sharon, Tawney, and Amanda asked me questions about my experience managing people and complex processes. I couldn't point to work experience in response to their questions, but I shared some of my leadership experiences throughout college as well as my mental model for how I approach complex problems. There were several times in the interview when Sharon exchanged a knowing glance with Tawney or Amanda in response to something I said, so I could tell they were with me in my thinking, but I had no idea who else had applied for the job, so I didn't put too much stock in it.

"Well, I tell ya, Nona," Sharon said while closing her notepad. "This has been such a delight. We have a few more candidates we're interviewing, so you will hear back on our decision within the next couple of weeks."

I left the interview with mixed emotions. It was evident from their questions that deeply understanding the processes they carried out was critical to the role, but I had no idea what those processes were, so I couldn't answer their questions intelligently. On the other hand, the energy of the interview was really positive, and we laughed a lot. It was a toss-up in my mind, so I was surprised and elated when I got the call that I had been selected for the role. I started my first official job out of college as the quality assurance analyst (QA) for the claims services department. I was responsible for all training and quality assurance for the team of processors servicing thousands of claims out of that department each day. I was part of a national team of six QAs, five of whom had risen through the ranks to assume that role after years working the many processes they were now assuring quality for. And there I was, fresh out of college having never done even *one* of the many processes. Sharon said she hired me because the confident way I answered the questions assured her I would "figure it out" if given the chance.

Her belief in me was far greater than my capabilities at the time, and I spent the first two months feeling as though I was a fraud and a failure. Who was *I* to tell someone how to do a job *I* didn't even know how to do? I was twenty-one, and the next youngest person in the department was in their early forties. I was young enough to be their daughter. During our weekly QA team planning calls, the "talk track" in my mind went something like, "Huh? What is she talking about? Wait, what in the *world* does ACP stand for? A what? What did she say? No, I can't get that report to you guys by the end of the week! I don't even know what that report is." But my lips would say, "Sounds good. Makes sense. Sure, I'll get the report to you by Friday." I felt wholly incompetent in my role and quickly realized that while my college degree had set me apart from many of the ladies doing the processing who never went to college, it hadn't prepared me to do my job.

As I felt more and more inadequate, I realized that one thing college *did* teach me to do was to study. And in a situation where I didn't know anything about anything, knowing how to think, learn, and work hard were the most important assets I had. When I first got into the role and asked what training I could take to learn the processes I would be auditing, I was told there was no formal training program in place. Each person was simply trained by another person who was there before them. There was no consistency, no formality, and no progression of training. As a result, the rate of errors was high because people often learned by trial and *error*. Some people even did things wrong unknowingly, and therefore trained people the wrong way. And those people trained other new people the wrong way. And that's the reason my role was created. After a couple of months of frustration and failure, I decided that instead of continuing to feel inadequate, I would build a training program that systematized the learning for all our processes.

It was a *massive* undertaking. There were more than a

hundred processes, requiring dozens of steps and a number of computer systems. I would come home from work every night with process manuals and handwritten workflow diagrams that were the result of discussions with longtimers who had helped talk me through the steps in each process. I would stay up late into the night, working while seated next to my husband as he watched the news. I took a Microsoft Visio class to learn how to map out all the processes in a way that was easy to follow. As I built each workflow and codified them in a training manual with instructions, screen shots, and discussion questions, my manager became more and more excited. She was so excited that, without telling me, she passed along my work to our director, who then scheduled a meeting with me to ask me to build out the same tools for the entire organization.

I had done the work simply to make myself more valuable to my team, but it had now gotten the attention of an executive, and my scope was broadened as a result. It wasn't that I was seeking more status or visibility. I was simply working to show Sharon that I was grateful for her faith in me. And gratefulness is the foundational mindset for a godly work ethic.

———— ◦◦◦◦ ————

Many people talk about their work with palpable antipathy. They describe it with a sigh, saying, "Well, it pays the bills," or they throw up their hands and say, "It's just a nine-to-five." We say "TGIF" because it signals the start of the weekend. But I believe God doesn't just give us a job to suffer through. I believe he gives us *territory* to lead. In Genesis 1:28 God said to Adam and Eve, "Be fruitful and increase in number; fill the earth and subdue it. Rule over the fish in the sea and the birds in the sky and over every living creature that moves on the ground." God didn't create us to passively participate in life; he created us to lead. First ourselves, then others. Leadership has been broadly misunderstood to equate to where your position sits on an organizational chart. Some people don't think of themselves as

> God doesn't just give us a job to suffer through. He gives us *territory* to lead.

leaders because they don't manage other people or because they don't chair a committee or have a big title. But leadership is not a question of position; it's a question of influence.

Have you ever been in a situation where "the leader," the one with the title and position, was undermined by someone they were "leading"? Perhaps the person intentionally worked against the boss in an effort to turn the hearts of people away, similar to how Absalom worked against his father, King David, in 2 Samuel 15. But in many cases, the undermining is unintentional and is simply the result of a leadership anointing on the person's life. If we back up a few decades from the story of Absalom, we can see this in the life of his father in relation to King Saul. King Saul disobeyed God, and in 1 Samuel 15, we find the prophet Samuel telling Saul that the Lord rejected him as king because of his disobedience. In the following chapter, Samuel anoints David as the new king of Israel, but interestingly enough, Saul was still on the throne while his successor, who didn't ask for the position, was chosen by God. David eventually ends up serving Saul, but God's favor on David's life makes the people's hearts turn toward him without him even trying. In this case, David's influence made him a leader whether he wanted to be or not.

As you reflect on your own life, can you see times when

you operated as a leader? Maybe people naturally gravitate toward you and ask you for guidance and input into their decisions regardless of whether you're their peer or their subordinate. This is leadership. Maybe you naturally see opportunities to make something better for your team or ways to make the load lighter for your own leader. Instead of having to be asked to do it or even having to run it by anyone, you just do it. This is leadership. You don't have to try to lead; you just do. This is the foundation of a godly work ethic.

Our work, our assignment, our territory should first honor God as a reflection of our gratitude to him for giving us the opportunity to represent him in the workplace. A godly work ethic shows itself in the attitude that every task, every decision, every assignment, and every action bears an opportunity to give God glory. For many of us, our lives and our work will be the only Bible our colleagues ever read. So the question we must ask ourselves is: If the way I show up at work—my attitude, my timeliness, my diligence, my integrity, my work quality—is the only testimony I could share with my colleagues, what would it say about my gratitude to God and the people who entrusted me with the assignment I now have?

> A godly work ethic shows itself in the attitude that every task, every decision, every assignment, and every action bears an opportunity to give God glory.

I was almost two years into my role and had gotten to a place where I was able to audit processes in my sleep. I enjoyed my regional and national team but started to think I wanted to take a different direction with my life—something that combined my love for community impact with my skill in communications. For the first time, I felt compelled to check job postings one afternoon. And there it was—a job that perfectly fit my skills and passions.

Nationwide had decided to make a major investment in community relations, and they were looking for someone to lead corporate community strategy for the southern region. I read through the job description excitedly because community engagement and service had been a passion of mine, and from what I could tell, they were hiring someone to do what I would have done for free. Then I read the minimum qualifications section, and my heart dropped. The role would sit on the executive leadership team and therefore required fifteen years of progressively responsible experience in community and public relations. I let out an audible sigh of disappointment, then closed the web browser and returned to work. My experience didn't come close to what was outlined as the minimum, so I decided it wasn't even worth considering. But just knowing the role existed gave me something to aspire to.

As I lay in bed that night, I couldn't get the job posting out of my head. I knew in my heart that I could do the job well if given a chance, but I also suspected there would be plenty of well-qualified applicants for such a high-level position. I prayed about it and asked God to give me wisdom and peace, then I fell asleep. When I woke the next morning, I knew I had to apply for the job. It was crazy and pretty much an impossibility, but I felt convinced that I needed to apply for it. I also knew I needed to take it another step further. Instead of applying for it and allowing the system to automatically reject me, I did something that would separate me from the undoubtedly crowded pool of candidates. I pulled together a pitch deck of ideas for the role and articulated a ninety-day strategy based on the goals outlined in the job description. I had the deck printed in color and bound, then I placed it on the chair of the hiring vice president and sent him an email that said:

> Good afternoon, Jack. I haven't had the pleasure of meeting you yet, but my name is Nona Jones, and I just applied for the open role on your team. I want to first acknowledge that I do not meet the minimum experiential qualifications for the job. I'm twenty-three years old, so fifteen years of experience would have required me to start working at eight. I would like you to know, however, that I have the vision, dedication, and work ethic to be successful in the role, and to demonstrate this, I have left a package on your desk chair for you to review. It would be a great honor to share my thoughts with you in person, so I hope to hear from you when convenient.

I heard from the director of human resources the next day, asking to schedule an interview. When I met with him, the look on his face was one of bemusement. Our interview went well, and he scheduled me for a second interview with Jack. Jack asked only a few questions, and I couldn't tell whether I answered right or wrong. The director of human resources scheduled me for another interview with a vice president at the home office in Columbus, Ohio, so I assumed I had done well enough to make it to the next step. When I met with her, she explained the context for the creation of the role and hinted at my being underqualified for it. I acknowledged that I wasn't qualified on paper but that

I had the ideas and tenacity to execute against the purpose the role was created for. She shook my hand at the end of the interview, and I returned to my desk pretty confident that I didn't get the job. I tried to wrap my mind around that reality, but two days later I got a call from the director of human resources congratulating me and offering me the job.

"Nona, I gotta tell you. I don't think anyone has ever done what you did in all my time here at the company. I've hired thousands of people, and no one has ever gone to those lengths to stand out from the competition. Jack was blown away by what you created and the ideas you laid out. He felt that was a sign of things to come. A very good sign."

———— ∞∞∞ ————

I couldn't believe I got the job. I was even *less* qualified for that job than the job I had in claims services. But I've come to believe that when we consistently show God that he can trust us to honor new, better opportunities, he will favor us in ways we can't even imagine.

One of the ways we can tell whether God can trust us is by asking ourselves whether we give our *all* or do we give *just enough* to get by? Do you approach your work with the goal of simply meeting expectations, or do you approach your work with the goal of making people see their expectations as too low for you? Many people want opportunities, but few people want to do the work. Getting those opportunities means consistently exceeding people's expectations of you, which requires doing more than the bare minimum.

Maybe you're an administrative assistant, and the expectation is that you'll simply manage your boss's work calendar and answer the phone. Instead, you research productivity apps that will integrate your boss's work schedule, personal schedule, travel schedule, and hobbies in one place so they can always know, at a glance, what's coming next in their life. And you don't just answer the phone. You get to know the birthdays of the people who call most frequently so you can send cards on behalf of your boss as a gesture of gratitude. Or maybe you work at a shoe store, and the only expectation is that you'll help people check out with their purchases. Instead, you get to know the customers who come in regularly by name and the type of shoes they like. When someone walks into the store, they hear you say, "Hey, Jim! We got a new pair of Birkenstocks that I think you'll enjoy. They'll be really comfortable for those weekend hikes."

Ecclesiastes 9:10 says, "Whatever your hand finds to do, do it with *all your might*, for in the realm of the dead, where you are going, there is neither working nor planning nor knowledge nor wisdom" (emphasis mine). This verse implores us to work hard because we have only one life to live. It encourages us to remember that at the end of this life, there will be no more chances to accomplish what we could have, should have, or would have. So we have to "leave it all on the field" with whatever our hand finds to do. Colossians 3:23 takes it a step further, saying, "Whatever you do, work at it with all your heart, as working for the Lord, not for human masters." If Jesus stepped out of heaven and into your living room right now and asked you to make him a peanut butter and jelly sandwich, you would probably assemble the best peanut butter and jelly sandwich ever made, complete with cutting the crusts off the bread, because the Lord Jesus asked you to do it. Yet as I mentioned earlier, God hasn't just given us a job; he's given us territory. And stepping up to lead our territory means summoning all the depth and width of human creativity and capacity. We have so much influence at our fingertips! We should treat the work we do as if Jesus asked us to do it because he is the one who called us to it.

I adopted a belief many years ago that every job I get to have is not a job; it's a paid internship. It's an opportunity to learn as much as I can and contribute as much as I can in the process. Many times we treat our jobs as places we go to "press play" on a daily routine of checking boxes. But while checking boxes may be part of

> Every job I get to have is not a job; it's a paid internship. It's an opportunity to learn as much as I can and contribute as much as I can in the process.

it, you can always learn something during the process. How we do our work says as much about us as the quality of the work we do, so we should strive to apply the highest level of integrity, consistency, and quality to what we do today because the habits we create today build the destiny we will inherit tomorrow.

———∞∞∞———

At twenty-seven years old, Jayson Blair became the subject of a national firestorm. The *New York Times* reporter was found to have committed so many acts of journalistic fraud that the paper had to issue a public apology on the front page of their iconic publication. Jayson made up interviews, scenes from stories, stole quotes from other papers, and even used details from photographs to fabricate having been somewhere he was not.

Jayson started at the paper as an intern, and his manager

noticed that he seemed to do more socializing than work, so she encouraged him to work for a smaller paper after he graduated. But he returned to the *New York Times* for an extended internship after what everyone assumed was his graduation. They would later find out that although he claimed to have graduated from college, he hadn't.

Jayson notoriously did his field reporting from behind a desk. Photographers who were assigned to do shoots with him said he would often tell them he was on his way but would never show up. Most of his stories had direct quotes that he lifted from other news outlets, often verbatim. One of the freelance photographers who was assigned to a story with him said he tried to reach Jayson by phone for more than twelve hours, but he kept making excuses for why they couldn't meet, so he eventually gave up.

One of the bedrock principles of journalism is truth, but Jayson cut so many corners in his reporting that it was impossible to know what was truth and what was a lie without going through the details one by one. Although his tenure at the *New York Times* was brief, the damage he did was deep and affected public faith in the iconic paper.

The way we show up for the assignments God gives us in our work can often have greater impact than only on us. The diligence we bring to the workplace can inspire diligence in others. But a lackadaisical attitude can similarly cause carelessness in others. Good success is born from leading ourselves first, and the way we lead ourselves inspires others. Good success leaves us fulfilled because it's the result of building strength of character through diligence, honesty, humility, and integrity. In contrast, the type of surface success we so often celebrate in our society is born from using others as opportunities to advance our own goals. It leaves us empty because while we may "achieve," we neglect what matters most—the people around us who we can inspire and encourage in their own gifts. Good success makes people want to be better and do better themselves, which means we must first lead ourselves well in the workplace in order to prove to God that we are worthy of the privilege of eventually leading others.

Chapter 11

Build Curiosity

"This loss ratio is concerning me," Jack said as he peered down at the stack of reports on the boardroom table in front of him. "John, do we have any more insight into what's going on there? It's almost twice as high as planned."

I was twenty-three and sitting in my first leadership team meeting in my new role at Nationwide. My boss, Jack, the regional vice president, was reviewing the week's profit and loss statement and relaying his concerns to the team.

"Yeah," said John, who led the claims division for the region. "We've had some large losses in the Panhandle that were abnormal for this time of year. Our forecasting had some wiggle room for the unexpected, but they were catastrophic and outside the model."

"I need an updated forecast. I would rather have a realistic view of how we'll end the year than hold out hope for hitting our initial projections. Get me that by end of day," Jack said as he continued thumbing through the spreadsheets in his packet.

I looked at the pieces of paper in front of me and saw a

foreign language. Every column was headed by an acronym I didn't understand, and every row was titled with a phrase I had never heard. Where every row and column met, there was either a decimal, percentage, or number that had no context. The rest of the group sitting around the boardroom table knew exactly what they were looking at, but I stared at it without knowing what I was supposed to do with the information. Jack asked more questions, then turned the time over to the team to share what was most important for their departments.

When it was my turn, he smiled at me and said, "Nona, what's happening in your world?"

I gave the group a high-level report of my thinking and priorities before inviting questions or feedback.

I left the meeting that day with countless pieces of paper and packets of information that were covered in what could have been hieroglyphics for all I knew. Listening to the conversations had felt like trying to decipher Africa's click language, Khoisan. Everyone nodded, smiled, and laughed at jokes with punch lines that went something like, "And that's when I said, 'What's the ACV!'" The room would erupt in uproarious laughter while I mustered a chuckle that sounded as confused as I felt. I realized right after that meeting that I was in over my head. Way over. I didn't even know what they were talking about, so how in the world would I be able to contribute anything valuable? My previous role had afforded me the time to learn and teach myself what I needed to know, but I was now part of a team of executives that moved quickly and didn't have time to bring me along.

I went through a couple more of those weekly meetings feeling utterly confused until I decided I wasn't satisfied with reporting on my piece of the pie without understanding how it related to everyone else's slice and, most important, the whole pie. I needed help. I didn't understand the language they were using, the goals they were measuring, or the unspoken interpersonal communications that drove so many of their interactions. But my insecurities wouldn't allow me to ask any questions in the team meetings or in my individual meetings with Jack. I didn't want them to wonder why I was at that table, so I knew I needed to show them that I deserved to be there.

When I got that job, I knew I was significantly underqualified, so I walked into it with that awareness hanging over my head. Although I had exuded confidence in the interviews, I was pretty sure I *wouldn't* get the job. But after I did, the weight of it settled on me, and I realized I had to perform. I had to meet the high expectations of the role because, just as Sharon had done in my prior role, Jack was taking a chance on me. I felt a deep responsibility to prove him right. As a result, I attended our leadership meetings without asking questions about the things I didn't understand. The confidence I had portrayed before I got the job was simply a mask for my insecurity.

When it comes to things we don't understand, insecurity has a way of making us act as if we have it all together when we really don't. Especially when we feel our reputation is on the line. Insecurity can make us feel as though we have to be seen as competent and in control, and as a result, we don't want to reveal our lack of understanding in an effort to maintain that facade. Maybe you got promoted to a management position and are now leading people who do things you don't understand, or perhaps you were asked to lead a project for a function you've never done before. In either case, the first instinct might be to "fake it 'til you make it," but many people who try this end up faking it 'til they *fail* it. Wisdom begins when we admit we *don't* have all the answers. The wisest people among us have a curiosity that compels them to seek understanding. And in a state of curiosity, we can begin the pursuit of wisdom.

> Wisdom begins when we admit we *don't* have all the answers.

Proverbs 4:7 says, "The beginning of wisdom is this: Get wisdom. *Though it cost all you have*, get understanding" (emphasis mine). The Word of God tells us that getting wisdom *and* understanding should be our utmost pursuit. But what is wisdom, and how is it different from understanding? And to go a bit deeper, how do they differ from the commonly used term *knowledge*? To unpack this, I want to begin with John 8:32, which says, "Then you will *know* the truth, and the truth will set you free" (emphasis mine). The Greek word for "know" used here is *ginosko*, which means "to get knowledge of, perceive." Knowledge, then, is what happens when we become *aware* of something. But becoming aware of something doesn't mean you understand it, right? If you began coughing uncontrollably one day, is awareness of your coughing enough to know why it's happening? No. For that next level of inquiry, we need to get *understanding*.

When I was growing up, I used to watch the G.I. Joe cartoon, and it always ended by saying, "Now you know. And knowing is half the battle." As I grew older, I wondered, "If knowing is *half* the battle, what is the other half?" I believe the other half of the battle is *understanding*. In Proverbs

4:7, the Hebrew word for understanding is *biynah*, which means, "the ability to judge well, being able to comprehend what is obscure." Understanding, then, goes beyond knowledge (awareness) in order to comprehend what you're now aware of. In the case of your cough, understanding would be gained by going to the doctor's office for an assessment. When they diagnose you with strep throat, you are now able to comprehend what's making you cough and, even more important, what you need to do to get healthy.

But even understanding is not enough, for in Proverbs 4:7 we are told to "get wisdom." The Hebrew word for "wisdom" used in verse 7 is *chokmah*, which means "skill." Skill is something we develop over time as we put our understanding into practice, so in instructing us to get "wisdom," God is telling us to get the byproduct of understanding-in-*action*.

> Wisdom that *lives out* knowledge and understanding leads to change.

It doesn't matter how many books you read on a subject. Until you put what you learn into practice, you will never develop skill. You may be knowledgeable, and you may have understanding, but you won't have skill because skill must be acquired through action. In the case of a strep throat diagnosis, wisdom happens when you take the medication to cure it. Wisdom that *lives out* knowledge and understanding leads to change.

Legend has it that one Sunday morning, a very frail man walked into a church service and made his way down the center aisle toward the pastor as he preached. Right before the man reached the platform, he passed out. A doctor who happened to be sitting nearby quickly assessed the man and told the pastor that the man was malnourished and needed food. The pastor asked for a sandwich to be quickly prepared and brought to the man from the church kitchen. Several people sat the man up and fanned him until he came to.

When he came to, the pastor said, "Sir, you just passed out here in our church. This doctor says we need to get you some food."

The man looked at the pastor and said, "Yeah, I'm hungry. I haven't eaten in a week."

The pastor said, "We're going to get you a sandwich, and once you eat it, you will feel better."

The man said, "Thank you so much."

At that very moment, an usher walked up with a sandwich and placed it in the man's frail hands.

"Sir," the pastor said, "the sandwich is in your hands. All you have to do is eat it."

The man said, "I know it's there!"

The pastor said, "Then eat it!"

The man stared blankly at the pastor until the pastor said, "Sir, if you don't eat that sandwich, you're going to die."

The man said with a hint of frustration, "Yeah, I know!"

The pastor asked, "Sir, do you want to die?"

The man responded, "Of course not."

The pastor and entire church said, "Eat the sandwich!"

The man said, "Look, I know I need to eat, and I know I'll die if I don't eat. I know I need to eat the sandwich and I know—"

Before he could finish his last sentence, he died, the uneaten sandwich still in his hands.

———⬡———

Knowledge and understanding in the absence of application is folly because wisdom is knowledge and understanding *in action*. Although this story is fictional, can you recognize times in your life when you have also fallen into the trap of not applying knowledge to your situation? Maybe your boyfriend yelled at you and even pulled back to hit you one day, so you knew he had violent tendencies. You even understood that it wasn't safe for you to stay with him. But you stayed anyway. Perhaps you stayed because of insecurities or economics, but after years went by and you finally *did* leave him, you realized none of those reasons were worth the pain you endured. Or maybe you were diagnosed as prediabetic and knew you couldn't eat sugary foods anymore. You even understood that if you didn't stop eating cakes, doughnuts, and cookies every day, you would become diabetic. But you kept eating those foods anyway. Perhaps you treated those foods as emotional crutches instead of dealing with some family issues that needed attention, but after getting the diagnosis and realizing your life was in jeopardy, you realized the food wasn't worth your life.

> Wisdom is knowledge and understanding *in action*.

Sometimes our lack of wisdom is simply the result of not seeing it modeled in our lives. We know *what* to do, but we don't know *how* to do it. In those times, when people know more than you do about the things you're supposed to know, wisdom will make you "pull up a chair" beside them to learn everything you can. This is often accomplished through the gift of mentorship, having someone in your life who has been where you are and can teach you *how* to put your goals into action. In the absence of a mentor, this can be accomplished through simply studying the lives of people who have achieved the thing you so desperately desire. Thankfully for me, I had such a gift within reach when I needed it most.

———— ⟨∞⟩ ————

"I don't know what any of this means," I said to Dianne as I placed a foot-high stack of papers on her desk. Dianne was a regular fixture at our leadership meetings and was often consulted when a report didn't make sense. I didn't know her well, but watching the confident way she explained what the numbers meant made me like her immediately. "When I look at this, all I see are rows and columns of random numbers and acronyms."

Dianne took a glance at the stack of papers, then looked up at me and said, "Nona, how old are you?"

"Twenty-three."

"Do you know how old I am?"

"No," I replied cautiously, not wanting to guess.

She smiled and said, "I'm old enough to be your mother. And so is everyone else on that team. We've all been at this for a long time. We've come up through the ranks and learned a lot along the way. You, my dear, just showed up out of the blue."

"Yeah. I know," I said.

"I'm not telling you this to make you feel bad. I'm telling you this to give you some perspective. You're clearly frustrated by what you don't know, but when I was your age and at the beginning of my career, I didn't know any of this either. It comes with time."

"I hear you, Dianne. But I don't have time. I'm already here now, and I don't have much room for error. I need to learn quickly."

Dianne looked at me with a kind, knowing smile, then walked over to a nearby bookcase and handed me a red book from her shelf.

"Here," she said. "You want to understand these reports, but before you try to understand those reports, you need to understand why those reports even matter."

I looked down at the book and saw *Good to Great* by Jim Collins prominently displayed on the cover. "What's this?"

"Nona, our CEO just issued the challenge to make this company the second largest property insurer in the nation in three years. We're not going to get there by doing what we've always done. Doing what we've done has gotten us to where we are *today*. But getting us to where we want to go is going to take something different. This book provides a new way of thinking about what lies ahead of us."

I thanked Dianne for the book and said, "Okay. So if I read this, will I start understanding the reports?"

"No," she said. "You will start understanding business. Come back and see me after you've read it, and we can go over the reports."

When I got home that night and opened the book, I couldn't put it down. The more I read, the more my curiosity was piqued. It chronicled the stories of companies that succeeded and failed and looked at the similarities and differences between the two. Collins also singled out some traits and trends that seemed to point to the makings of a great company. He also provided practical tips, tools, and tactics to help company leaders make the shift from good to great personally, and it was in those teachings that I found the greatest sense of inspiration. In outlining what he calls "Level 5 Leaders," Collins showed people who had both intense professional resolve combined with inspiring personal humility. In those pages I saw an aspiration for myself and, even more, an understanding of why the numbers mattered so much. The numbers helped us navigate toward our business's north star by acting as benchmarks to which our goals and performance could be anchored and, later, measured.

I returned to Dianne's office a few days later, my anxiety replaced by excitement. "I get it. I don't get the acronyms or the numbers, but I get why they matter. And I'm willing to do the hard work to understand my role in driving them."

"Excellent," she said. "Now, let's get started."

With a red pen she spelled out every acronym on the page. When she finished, she said, "All right, now your next step is to define these terms."

"I thought that's what you were going to do."

She laughed. "Nona, my defining them for you will only make you reliant on me. You have to learn this stuff for yourself."

"Okay, but where can I go to get the definitions?"

"Try the bookstore. Business and management section."

I went to the bookstore after work that day, and the moment I stepped into the business section, I felt as if I had stepped into Oz. There were books about any and every business topic I could have wanted, from financial management to leadership to hiring and more. I saw a book called *The 360 Degree Leader* by John Maxwell that purported to teach how to lead up, across, and down, so I grabbed that book as my first selection. I then saw a book called *What the CEO Wants You to Know* by Ram Charan, and I figured I couldn't go wrong with that one. By the time I finished grabbing books and checking out, I had spent more than three hundred dollars on ten titles. And I felt great. A book on business financials discussed the various financial ratios used to measure the fiscal health of a company, and having always been a math lover, I worked through the formulas, which made everything click in a new way.

By the time I returned to Dianne, I was able to tell her what all the acronyms meant and what they measured. I had some contextual questions that were specific to the insurance industry, but she was proud of what I had done. When I told her I bought ten books in one day, she laughed and said, "Nona, you've now discovered the secret to success. And it's publicly available. Never stop learning. Never stop asking questions. And if you don't know something, pick up a book. Read everything you receive for meetings. Everything. Most people show up to meetings completely unprepared, but if you do the hard work and learn the information, you will be the most prepared. And being prepared is the most powerful weapon you will have in business."

⸺ ❀❀❀ ⸺

In a January 2018 *Time* magazine article, Bill Gates said, "There's never been a better time to be alive if you're curious." The man who built Microsoft into one of the largest, most successful companies in history had dropped out of Harvard in the 1970s to pursue his vision of computing. But despite dropping out of school, he never stopped learning. In fact, Gates has said, "I'm a weird dropout because I take college courses all the time."[1] Gates has attributed his success to being a lifelong student, not just of computing but of everything. His curiosity about that which he doesn't yet know has led him to spend most of his life reading for an hour every day, racking up fifty books per year every year.

Although he stepped down from his day job at Microsoft, Gates never stopped his learning regimen because "you don't really start getting old until you stop learning. Every book teaches me something new or helps me see things differently. Reading fuels a sense of curiosity about the world, which I think helped drive me forward in my career."

Bill Gates was named the youngest billionaire in history in 1987 at the age of thirty-one, but with a net worth of more than $100 billion dollars more than thirty years later, he still sees himself as a student. A student of life, the world, and business.

———— ∞∞∞ ————

If a man who is the definition of success incarnate still believes he has more to learn, building curiosity and pursuing wisdom should become part of our success regimens. If you're a parent and you know spanking as the only disciplinary technique, perhaps attending a parenting conference in your area might broaden your understanding of other ways to encourage the right behavior instead of only punishing the wrong behavior. If you've never been out of the country because you don't have the money, perhaps a visit to the travel section of your local library can expose you to the sights of faraway lands. If you're just getting started in your career and don't know much about your company or industry, perhaps enrolling in an industry-specific professional certification program will give you a higher level of understanding about your role and value to the organization.

As I was sharpening my own knowledge base in my role at Nationwide, I was approached with the opportunity of pursuing a professional designation called the Chartered

Property and Casualty Underwriter (CPCU). It's the highest credential of the property and casualty insurance industry, and most of the chief-level executives at Nationwide had it. It usually took two to four years to achieve it, but I was encouraged to enroll because of the potential people saw in me. And I almost did. But as I prayed and thought about my future, I determined that it would be better for me to understand business in general than to spend years of my life understanding one industry. It was at that point that I decided to pursue a Master of Business Administration, and that degree has proven invaluable across my professional, ministerial, and entrepreneurial ventures.

If you don't know, ask. If you can't ask, read. There will always be more questions than answers in life and business, but that's what keeps it interesting. We can't be successful at something we don't know how to do, but once we learn how to do it, we must remember whom we're doing it for.

Chapter 12

Build Faith

As my career continued to blossom in the private sector, I was asked to join the public sector to lead the local, state, and federal legislative and community affairs team for a multiservice utility. Although I had no former experience in public policy, I quickly grew to love it and, a few years in, caught the attention of the CEO of a large nonprofit serving at-risk girls in Florida. I was asked to take the role of chief external affairs officer, and I built the organization's first federal legislative strategy. Given my personal story of trauma, I brought a level of passion and intensity to my advocacy on behalf of marginalized girls that led to invitations to speak at conferences and events.

A couple of years into the role, I received an unbelievable call from the United States Department of Justice asking me to keynote Attorney General Loretta Lynch's National Youth Violence Prevention Summit, an event that drew elected and appointed leaders from all fifty states as well as Congress to hear the latest ideas on how best to serve at-risk youth. National statistics showed at the time that while overall juvenile delinquency rates were going down, delinquency rates for *girls* were going up. And unlike boys, who had a well-documented correlation between school dropouts and prison (i.e., the school-to-prison pipeline), research showed that *eight out of ten* girls in the juvenile justice system had been *sexually abused*. Addressing delinquency in girls meant dismantling a sexual-abuse-to-prison pipeline.

When the day came, I stepped onto the brightly lit stage at the summit and walked toward the center. I briefly looked out into the darkened audience of almost one thousand elected and appointed officials at the local, state, and federal levels of government from across the country, then said, "Today a baby girl will be born, and when her brand new eyes finally adjust and focus, she will meet the loving gaze of her mother and father, who will be awestruck by her immediately evident brilliance and beauty. And they will instantly agree that they will stop at nothing to make sure that their daughter realizes and unleashes her potential on the world. And in that same hospital, another newborn girl will lie in the nursery crying. Uncomforted. The unwanted byproduct of a young mother's search for validation with a guy who used her body as a waste receptacle for his own dysfunction. These two baby girls are equally vulnerable, but one will leave the hospital and go home to a protective, supportive environment, while the other baby girl will be raised to fear the darkness of night because in the dark . . . that's where she's violated by her mother's many boyfriends."

I was the only speaker that day who was talking about the unique issues facing vulnerable girls, and I had been invited to make my case to the room of legislators and agency heads because there was still little awareness about what girls are experiencing. You could have heard a *feather* drop as I spoke. No one's face was aglow with their laptop or phone; everyone's eyes were on me, and their ears were open. I had only twelve minutes to share my message that day, so instead of a highly produced, over-designed presentation, I simply shared my heart. I shared myself.

I wanted to bring the point home, so I said, "As I close, I want to share a true story. A girl was born to a mother who didn't even want her, and the girl was sexually abused by her mom's boyfriend between the ages of five and eleven. She told her mom what happened, but after having him arrested, her mom brought him back home on the day of his release, and the abuse continued. She started acting out in school and was labeled as a problem child at an early age and was told she had behavioral and learning disabilities, but through the grace of God, her middle-school teachers saw beyond her behavior and recognized her potential. They didn't know what was happening to her at home, but their affirmation transformed the young girl's life dramatically. She focused on her schoolwork and excelled. She entered college as a first-year sophomore on a full academic scholarship. She eventually earned a master's of business administration and completed studies at Harvard Law School, becoming a corporate executive at a Fortune 500 company at the age of twenty-three. And the reason I know this story so well is because that little girl was me." The room erupted in applause, and when the applause settled, I left everyone with the challenge of seeing beyond a girl's behavior and speaking to her potential because that was the *only* reason why I was standing in front of them. I was a product of grace.

As I made my way off the stage and reached my seat, a beautiful black woman walked up to me and said, "That was amazing. Will you be around later? I want to speak with you." I said yes as she hugged me and smiled, then walked away. A few minutes later she was on stage introducing the next speaker, her best friend and senior advisor to President Obama, Valerie Jarrett. I didn't know it at the time, but the woman who hugged me was United States Assistant Attorney General Karol Mason. After conducting the conversation with Jarrett, she found me, and we talked for only a few minutes, as she was needed for other parts of the program. She gave me her cell number and told me to call her whenever I needed to. I was amazed. I couldn't believe that a woman who oversaw an annual budget of $4 billion, who had direct access to the president of the United States and the type of power and influence most people only read about, would make time to connect with me. But it wouldn't be the first or the last time. She has become a trusted friend, advisor, confidante, and mentor.

When I returned to the office after the event, I was on a personal high. I had made sure to lift up and amplify the work of our nonprofit as a national case study in what can happen when public investment is made in proven solutions, so countless mayors, state legislators, and federal agency heads had asked me to contact them about expanding our organization to their municipalities. I was eager to follow up and build on the momentum. But the moment I walked into our executive team meeting that morning, I felt something was off. We discussed the usual topics: funding, program performance, staffing, and legislative impact. But when it came time to provide my departmental update, I sensed a "cooling" in the room. I didn't know what it was or why I felt that way, but the excitement with which I shared about the summit was tempered by the looks of irritation on several of their faces. When I left the meeting, a person I was close to asked to go to lunch. After we ordered our food, she said, "Nona, I need to tell you something."

I thought she was going to tell me she was leaving, but instead she said, "You have some haters working against you."

"Haters? What do you mean?"

"Well, I was in a meeting about your coming to speak to the team, and we were told you probably wouldn't have time because you were only interested in jetting off to the White House."

I knew who had said it—someone who also had a high-level role on the executive team. I said, "Wait. What?"

"Yeah. I know. And it was the *way* it was said. With an eye roll and attitude. It was clear to me that she's jealous of you."

"Jealous . . . of *me*? For doing my *job*?"

"No, not jealous of you for doing your job. Jealous of you for doing your job *well*. And that's not all." Apparently, someone else on the executive team had been working behind the scenes to make sure my budget was slashed for the following year.

"Why would she be doing that?" I asked.

"Nona, you're outshining them. And they don't want you to win. They've been planting seeds about you, saying you're building your own empire instead of the organization's."

I was dumbfounded. Everything I had ever done was because I believed so strongly in the mission. Although I was the face of the work because of my externally facing role, there was never a question in my mind about the ultimate goal being to advance the organization. But it finally made sense. The cold atmosphere in the executive team meeting that morning was the result of the toxic feelings my colleagues had been nursing about me. And out of jealousy they had been actively working to turn my boss and others against me. I left lunch that day feeling confused, hurt, and outnumbered. These women had been at the organization longer than I had and were the first people my boss hired, so their allegiance to each other was tight. I knew nothing would break that allegiance, and I felt sad because I had planned to be at that organization for the rest of my career.

The discomfort of the situation led me to seek God for guidance, but I had no idea he was about to teach me what trusting him beyond reason really looks like. What *faith* looks like.

Many of us say we have faith in God, but how many of us have ever had to *truly* trust him beyond our control? Our prayers tend to ask God to bless our plans instead of seeking him for his. Maybe you've done this before. You applied for the job you wanted, *then* asked God to give you favor to get it. But was that job his perfect will for you despite the impressive title, large salary, and corner office? Or you fell in love with a new man who doesn't believe in the neces-

> Faith requires seeking God *before* making a decision.

sity of church, *then* asked God to change his heart and make him attend church with you. But was that man God's perfect will for you despite the butterflies you get every time you stare into his eyes? So many of our prayers happen *after* we've already made a decision without seeking God, but faith requires seeking God *before* making a decision.

In my case, so much of what I had accomplished in my

life and career up until that time hadn't required much faith. I applied for the job I wanted out of college and got it. I applied for the next job and got it. I was recruited for the one after that and recruited, again, for the one after that and recruited, again, for the one after that. In every case I would pray to God to give me favor, but my prayers amounted to nothing more than asking God to sprinkle some "holy fairy dust" over *my* plans instead of seeking him for *his*. I was four years into this job and loved it. I planned to be in it for at least twenty more years. I had no intention of changing anything. But the day I prayed and asked God to help me understand what was going on, I heard the Spirit say, "This assignment is over." I was confused. How could an assignment be over when I planned on staying in it for another couple of decades? I prayed again and "this assignment is over" settled over my spirit again, this time with a level of finality that let me know I had heard correctly. But I was entirely perplexed. What would I do next? I hadn't thought one time about leaving my job in the four years I was in it, so what was my next move?

For the first time in my life, I prayed and earnestly sought God for direction. I wasn't asking God to bless a premade plan; I was asking God for instruction. And what he said left me even more confused. The Spirit told me to resign at the end of the fiscal year, June 30. It was mid-April at the time, so that would have given me less than two months to plan my departure. I prayed and asked God whether I could stay through the end of the year to give me some time, but his instruction never changed. June 30. I mentally and emotionally prepared myself to tell my husband what God had said, knowing the conversation was going to be very hard. He had gone into full-time ministry a year earlier, and we lost half his salary because the church couldn't afford to pay him what he had been making. My salary absorbed the loss, so we didn't have to change our lifestyle. But we had two small children in private school by then, as well as a new home, so when I told him God told me to resign from my job, he asked, "Uh . . . are the bills resigning too?"

With a quickened heartbeat and tight throat, I said, "I don't know, honey . . . but I do know that this is what the Lord said. And it's what I have to do."

He gave me a look that said "yeah, right," but he saw in my eyes that I was serious, so he said, "Well, I know this much. If God said it, he will provide."

Neither of us had any idea what God was about to provide.

I was a nervous wreck. I had my letter of resignation in a sealed envelope addressed to my boss, and we were set to meet at 1:00 p.m. We were out of town together at a conference, so I asked her to meet me at the hotel restaurant. The culture of the executive team had continued to deteriorate over the past two months, so even when I began to think, "Maybe I heard this wrong. I can stick it out," something would happen that kept me on track. I arrived in the restaurant around 12:50 p.m. to settle my nerves, but I was shaking, something that had never happened to me before. When I saw my boss round the corner of the restaurant and spot me in the back, I felt a bit lightheaded. Thoughts of "What are you doing? Are you *sure* you heard right? Are you *sure* that wasn't just your emotions speaking?" raced through my head, and as she sat down, my usual easy way of making small talk melted into a series of awkward swallows of water.

I stumbled and stammered through a few of her light-hearted observations about the conference before I said, "The reason I asked you to meet with me today is because I'm resigning from my position." I slid the envelope containing my letter across the table as the color left her face.

"Resigning? What? Why?"

"The culture on the executive team has become toxic. I've shared my thoughts and concerns with you before, and I haven't sensed a change. So after prayer and consideration, I feel God is leading me to pursue other opportunities."

"Well, is there anything I can do to make you change your mind? I mean . . . this is . . . big."

"No. My decision is final. I've already prepared a transition plan. My last day will be July 14."

"July 14! That's only two weeks. You have so much work in motion. Can we have more time?"

"When we get back to the office Monday, I'll walk you through where everything stands. I've been preparing for the last couple of months to ensure everything has a smooth handoff."

"Wow," she said. "I . . . I wasn't expecting this. Well, what are you going to do next? I would definitely want to let everyone know when I announce that you're leaving."

My decision was being made in faith. I hadn't even thought of that question, so when I said, "I'll tell you soon," I wasn't sure what I would be telling her.

We finished speaking around 1:40 p.m., and I walked to the hotel concierge desk to have them retrieve my luggage and bring my car around. As I drove away, the hotel got smaller and smaller in my rearview mirror. I felt both a lightness and a heaviness in my heart. I felt light because I knew I was following God's perfect will for me, but I also felt heaviness because I was now swimming in completely uncharted territory. I said, "All right, Lord. Now what?" and merged onto the highway for the five-hour drive home. At 2:05 p.m., my phone rang with an unfamiliar 650 area code that said "San Francisco." I figured it was a telemarketer and decided not to answer it, then I heard the Spirit say, "Take that call."

"Hello?"

"Yes, is this Nona Jones?" a woman's voice asked.

"Yes . . . who is this?"

"Hi! I'm calling from Facebook," she said with an audible smile.

"Facebook? Facebook doesn't call people. Who is this for real?"

"No, really. I'm calling from Facebook. Listen, I don't know if you know this, but last week Mark changed the mission of our company to focus on community building. One of the largest communities is the community of faith, and we've never focused on them before. I was given your name as someone to talk to about helping us with this work. Would you be interested?"

My mind was still in a fog from having resigned from my job twenty-five minutes earlier, so I thought she was asking me to join a committee or advisory board when I said, "Okay. Just email me some information, and I'll review it over the weekend. We can talk again Monday."

When I walked into my house five hours later, I unpacked my luggage and showered, then walked into my office to check my email. As soon as the browser refreshed, I saw an email from Facebook with a subject heading about a job.

I called to my husband in the other room and said,

"Babe . . . Facebook just emailed me a job description to lead their global strategy for communities of faith."

"Why would they do that?" he asked.

I said, "I have no idea."

When I clicked the link and read the job description, my heart leaped with amazement and excitement, but then I saw the job was in Menlo Park, California, and thought, "Oh. Well, I guess that's out." My husband and I had decided at the beginning of our marriage that we weren't moving from Gainesville, Florida, because that's where his father's church was, and my husband knew he would eventually be senior pastor someday.

"Never mind, babe," I said. "It would require us to move to California."

He said, "Yeah. I guess that's a no."

By the time Monday came around, I knew I had to tell the lady thank you for thinking of me, but I couldn't move. Yet there was something in me that wanted to do the job. It wasn't that it was Facebook; it was that the job would enable me to equip leaders of faith to use Facebook for ministry. I saw in the job an opportunity to revolutionize the way "church" was done, and even though I had never worked in tech or social media, I had a background in ministry.

"Thanks so much for thinking of me," I said into the phone. "I see the position is based in California, and I can't move, so unfortunately, I won't be able to take this job."

"Well," she said, "we have a policy that you have to live where your position is located, but we believe you're the right person for this, so we'll make it work."

"You'll make it . . . work? What does that mean?"

"We can figure out an arrangement where you don't have to move. Maybe you can come to headquarters once a month or a few days out of the month. I don't know. I *do* know you're the right person, though, so we will figure it out. Want to move forward?"

Two weeks later, on the last day in my job, I received my official offer letter from Facebook—for a job I never applied for. Twenty-five minutes after I resigned, in faith and obedience to God, from the job I loved, he blessed me with a job I would have never dreamed of because I wouldn't have thought it was possible. But that's how our God is. Ephesians 3:20 says that God is able to do exceedingly, abundantly above all that we ask or think. This means God is able to do more than we can even *imagine* is possible. And he meets our faith at our level of obedience.

Abraham is often called the "Father of Faith" because in Romans 4:18–21, the Bible says,

> Against all hope, Abraham *in hope* believed and so became the father of many nations, just as it had been said to him, "So shall your offspring be." Without weakening in his faith, he faced the fact that his body was as good as dead—since he was about a hundred years old—and that Sarah's womb was also dead. Yet he *did not waver through unbelief* regarding the promise of God, but was *strengthened in his faith* and gave glory to God, being *fully persuaded* that God had power to do what he had promised. (emphasis mine)

Although Abraham never wavered in his faith that God would bring his promise to pass, Abraham's faith remained intact even when God asked the unthinkable. After trusting and believing God to provide him with a son and *finally* receiving that promise in Isaac, God said to Abraham, "Take your son, your only son, whom you love—Isaac—and go to the region of Moriah. Sacrifice him there as a burnt offering on a mountain I will show you" (Genesis 22:2). The Bible speaks matter-of-factly about what happened next, saying, "Early the next morning Abraham got up and loaded his donkey. He took with him two of his servants and his son Isaac" (Genesis 22:3). Let me give you my "Mommy Translation" of this verse. "So Abraham couldn't sleep all night through the tears and heartache of what God had said. He begged and pleaded with God for another sacrifice. He rent his clothes and covered himself in sackcloth and ashes out of mourning. But God confirmed that his will was unchanged. At the brink of psychosis, Abraham pulled himself together, saddled his donkey, and took two of his young men with him, as well as his beloved, highly-prized son, Isaac. The one he would have exchanged places with if God would have allowed it."

No parent can imagine killing their own child, the child they prayed and fasted for during years and years of barrenness. Yet God was asking Abraham to sacrifice the one thing he loved above all else to prove his faithfulness. I believe God is asking us to do the same. He isn't asking us to sacrifice our children, but he *is* asking us to sacrifice our ambitions. Our dreams. Our plans. Our desires. Our wills. God is asking us to lay all that on the altar because until we lay our need to control our lives on the altar, we can't operate in faith. Abraham has been called the "Father of Faith" because he exercised a level of trust in God that was irrational, nonsensical, and unexplainable. Hebrews 11:6 says, "Without faith it is impossible to please him: for he that cometh to God must believe that he is, and that *he is a rewarder of them that diligently seek him*" (KJV, emphasis mine). Maybe you've felt God telling you to leave the boyfriend you've been with for years, but the thought of being alone makes you stay. Trust God and leave. Maybe you've known God intends for you to open a bakery, but you've never run a business, so you remain in your desk job. Trust God and open it. Maybe you know God wants you to serve in the children's ministry, but you're afraid to do it because you've never had children yourself. Trust God and serve.

> Surrender your plans to his hands.

God meets our faith at our level of obedience. I'm a living witness that when we trust God in irrational, non-sensical, and unexplainable ways, he can show his irrational, nonsensical, and unexplainable favor in our lives. But only if you learn to surrender your plans to his hands.

Chapter 13

Build Love for People

The most rewarding part of my professional journey has been being able to invest in the leadership journeys of others. But if I'm honest, I didn't always think that way. One of the most important leadership lessons I've learned in my career is that insecurities have the power to make you neglect your primary responsibility as a leader—to love the people you lead.

———— ∞ ————

"She said she's leaving because you don't care about her."

About three years into my chief-level role at the nonprofit, my boss called to tell me my star employee had told her she was planning on resigning because of me. I was dumbfounded.

"Wait. She said she's leaving because of . . . *me?* I knew she wouldn't be around forever because she's so talented and ambitious, but I never would have guessed she would leave because of me."

"Yeah. That's what she said. What do you want to do?"

"I want to talk with her. Can we arrange to have her come to town for a sit-down with me, you, and her?"

"Okay. I'll ask her to make the trip."

When I hung up the phone, I was stunned. Jennifer was brilliant, confident, and self-sufficient. She led the state legislative affairs work for my team, and I trusted her decision-making ability so much that I tried to stay out of her way and let her do her job however she saw fit. She was one of the people on my team who I didn't have any concerns about because I trusted her to do her job with excellence. I thought the world of her in my head and heart, but something in my actions communicated to her that I didn't care about her.

She wasn't quitting only her *job*. She was quitting *me*.

I had terminated employees before her because of poor performance or breaches of ethical standards, but this was the first time in my career that I had an employee leave me voluntarily because they felt I wasn't a good leader. As I reflected on the relationship I thought I had with Jennifer, I soon realized where I had misstepped. Because she was self-sufficient, I had neglected her almost entirely.

Jennifer worked remotely in a city almost three hours from our headquarters. I felt fortunate to have inherited her when I was first hired, and I noticed her talent immediately. At the first opportunity I had, I promoted her. We met by phone every two weeks to catch up on her work and to keep her abreast of my priorities, but I rarely visited her in person. I made the trip to the state capital where she lived a few times a year, but mostly to meet with legislators or agency heads. We would have lunch before the meetings to make sure I was briefed and prepped to move the needle on whatever item we needed to advocate for, but after those meetings ended, I would climb back into my car and head back home. I invested no time in the relationship beyond the work, and by doing that, I communicated to her that I didn't care about her.

To make matters worse, I mistakenly thought she wasn't attending an event our organization was hosting because it was happening at the start of legislative session. But to my surprise, she showed up, and I said, "Hey, Jennifer! I didn't think you'd be here." What I meant to convey was that I was pleasantly surprised by her attendance, but it landed in her already hurt heart as my not wanting her there. I didn't know it at the time, but she conveyed all of that and more through tear-filled eyes when we finally sat down to talk.

"I went back to my room and cried. I felt dismissed by you," she said through tears. "I feel like there's no connection between us. I really admired you and was so excited when I found out you were going to be my boss. But it's felt like you don't want me here. And that's why I'm leaving."

"Jennifer, let me first apologize to you. I am truly, truly sorry for making you feel that way. The truth is that I've always viewed you as one of the strongest people on my team. And I now see that I overlooked some important opportunities to demonstrate that to you. I know you've already accepted another job, but I want you to know that I appreciate you and feel blessed to have had you on my team. I'm so sorry that we didn't get to have this conversation earlier because I would have loved the chance to show you how important you are and have been to me. Suffice it to say that I will always be here for you to help you in any way I can."

After she left the room, my boss turned to me and said, "I'm really impressed with how you handled that. I've been in meetings like that before, and it usually turns into a shouting match. I think she needed to hear what you said. I hope you feel good about that talk. You should."

But I didn't. And I still don't, years later. I believe that no matter how much you achieve numerically, none of it matters if you fail people emotionally. Success should be measured by the degree to which we achieved our goals while ensuring that the people who helped us along the way feel loved, respected, supported, and valued.

> No matter how much you achieve numerically, none of it matters if you fail people emotionally.

This situation with Jennifer played out right in the middle of a particularly successful season of my life. My work on behalf of the organization had placed me on the radar of key high-level leaders in the Obama administration. I was regularly being invited to the White House for convenings on critical policy issues in the juvenile justice and education space. I was traveling around the country delivering keynote talks at many of the largest conferences for youth and families. I had secured millions of dollars in new corporate funding and had even secured the organization's first multiyear, multimillion-dollar federal grant. I was making a lot of headway with the Georgia legislature to get an appropriation passed that would expand our footprint to another state, and I was leading the organization through a major rebrand. My boss had even asked me whether I had any aspirations to be CEO of the organization someday. But the problem with all this is found in one letter: I.

Although I was leading a cross-functional team of

high-performing leaders in their own right, I was often acting as a one-woman show. I didn't micromanage people because I trusted they were the best for their job, but I wasn't managing them either. My hands-off approach made some of the people on my team feel disconnected from me, and Jennifer was the first to bite the dust. When I thought about it, I realized that my work ethic was operating at maximum capacity, but it was being fueled by the same dark side of me that had motivated my success in high school. The parts of me that were insecure took my worth from the external validation of achievements and fueled my ambition to achieve more goals at the expense of the people I needed to achieve them. People such as Jennifer.

Perhaps you can relate. Have you ever been so focused on achieving something that you sacrificed time with your friends and loved ones to achieve it? Maybe someone you cared about experienced a death in their family, but instead of rearranging your work schedule or personal plans to support them at the funeral, you told them, "I can't make it right now. I'll take you out to lunch later." Maybe your son plays sports on Saturdays, and instead of arranging your schedule to attend the games, you wake up every Saturday morning and get dressed to head into the office with the goal of getting a head start on next week's work. If we take a moment to think about it, there have probably been times when we prioritized an achievement over a relationship, but I've

> Success that requires sacrificing relationships isn't success at all.

come to believe success that requires sacrificing relationships isn't success at all.

The key to building a love for people is to understand that people receive love in different ways. Gary Chapman has a brilliant book titled *The 5 Love Languages*, which explains the different ways people receive love. Some people receive it through acts of service and some through words of affirmation. Others receive it through gifts, and still others receive it through physical touch. As I stepped back from the situation, I realized Jennifer's love language was quality time, and I *never once* prioritized making *quality* time for her. I would breeze in and out of town for meetings she arranged on my behalf, but because I didn't understand that quality time was her love language, I never carved out the time to simply be in her world and get to know her as a person. That was such a missed opportunity, and as I listened to her heart the day she tearfully shared how she felt, I realized it all went back to my not speaking her love language. I constantly affirmed her and my other staff members through words and would greet them all with hugs when I saw them, but she needed more. She needed my time.

In addition to my time in general, she needed time with me to do our work together. In hindsight, I should have had her with me at every White House meeting and every meeting at the Georgia state legislature. Instead, I often left her out of the loop of my work in favor of plowing ahead without having to pause and bring her along with me. But love doesn't prioritize progress over people.

> Love doesn't prioritize progress over people.

This concept is beautifully shown by Jesus in Luke 15:4–6, where he says to the Pharisees, "Suppose one of you has a hundred sheep and loses one of them. Doesn't he leave the ninety-nine in the open country and go after the lost sheep until he finds it? And when he finds it, he joyfully puts it on his shoulders and goes home. Then he calls his friends and neighbors together and says, 'Rejoice with me; I have found my lost sheep.'" Love isn't satisfied with 99 percent of the group being okay. Love seeks out the 1 percent too. And that requires a belief that people are more important than prizes.

Had I simply included Jennifer in my work, she would have felt validated and appreciated. She would have felt as though she mattered and was an integral part of the strategy. And if I had stepped out of my world into hers, she would have felt affirmed and prioritized. But when we allow success to perch us too highly above the people we are privileged to lead, we can forget the need to love people, because we're too busy looking down on them.

His brilliance was legendary. Thought leaders lauded him as the greatest businessman the world had ever seen, despite being a college dropout. After cofounding Apple Computers in the midseventies, Steve Jobs rose from obscurity to lead the world's largest, most successful company in history. He and his partner, Steve Wozniak, turned the novel idea of personal computers into a global phenomenon, and Jobs achieved great fame, prestige, and notoriety along the way. But despite the external indicators of success, his journey to prominence was riddled with scandal and turbulence.

In 1985, after several years of losing to emerging competitors in the computing market, Steve Wozniak left the company he cofounded, citing it had "been going in the wrong direction for the last five years."[1] A peek under the hood of the company found Steve Jobs fighting with other leaders in the company and working to pressure them to support his vision for the future. But with financials rapidly declining for the products he championed, combined with his increasingly notorious temper flares at staff, Apple's board of directors stripped him of his duties and ousted him as leader. Business historians have noted that the deterioration in financial results was the main motivation behind his firing, not his behavior toward employees.

Twelve years later, in the summer of 1997, Apple underwent another leadership shift after the board fired then CEO Gil Amelio, and Steve Jobs returned as interim CEO. With his return to the helm of the organization, he set what appeared to be a new tone for the organization, one that was rooted in partnership instead of competition with longtime rival Microsoft. He introduced a number of sleek, new products to the market, including the iMac and iBook, smashing prior computer sales records with each release. He also led the company through the launch of retail stores, along with the iPod, iTunes, iPhone, and iPad. Over the next fourteen years, his vision turned Apple into the global computing leader, and his success was canonized in countless awards and recognitions. But while the world viewed him as a genius, the people who worked for him characterized him as a monster.

Steve was reported to regularly yell at people without provocation, degrade hospitality and restaurant staff, double-park in handicapped spaces, and cut in front of employees at lunchtime. He is even quoted as saying to Denise Young Smith, who was interviewing for the role of Apple's head of human resources, "I've never met one of you who didn't suck. I've never known an HR person who had anything but a mediocre mentality." His propensity to tell employees they and their work sucked is well documented, and cofounder Steve Wozniak said, "Some of the most creative people in

Apple who worked on the Macintosh left the company and refused to ever again work for Jobs."[2]

In his quest for perfection, Steve Jobs destroyed many of the people who worked alongside him to make Apple what it is today. The level of anxiety, depression, and humiliation they felt has been noted in countless stories of what it was like to work at Apple during his time as CEO. He resigned from Apple in August 2011 and died from pancreatic cancer just two months later in October 2011. As people were reflecting on his life, the standard recollection of his business prowess was immediately undercut by the way he treated the people who helped him build his business.

Instead of a legacy of greatness, his legacy is tinged by behavior that prioritized progress over people. Despite the many contributions

> Good success requires seeing *people* as the end.

he made to the world, the people who worked alongside him are still healing from the emotional and psychological trauma he caused.

The pursuit of success can easily blind you to the purpose of success—leaving the world better off than you found it. The achievements we accumulate to our own credit make for a nice obituary, but the ways we use our life to lift another person higher build an enduring legacy. As tempting as it sometimes is to use people as means to an end, good success requires seeing *people* as the end. When you consider the goals you're pursuing, how many of them will leave others better off than when you met them? And as you build your own career or business or platform, how many others are you taking along with you for the ride? If the only person who can look back and see a benefit from the work of your hands is you, you will build an impressive monument to yourself, but no one will be standing with you to celebrate what was erected. When we love people and prioritize them above ourselves, we will always win, even if it requires us to lose.

I recently chose to resign from a professional organization I had been president of for the last several years, because my work and ministry schedule was crowding out the time I had to spend with my children. I was torn about the decision because I loved the organization and had been encouraged to consider serving at the national level. But when I counted the cost of staying in the organization, my decision became clear and easy. I could have continued to spend hours each week preparing for meetings or attending meetings or resolving issues that arose, or I could spend those hours with my little boys, watching their favorite program or reading a book or going to the zoo. I realized that when I reach my death bed, I won't regret having not served in a national office of that organization. But I *will* regret not spending time with my children that can never be recovered. It wasn't about my achieving another bullet on my resume. It was about my creating lasting memories with the ones who matter most.

What tough decisions do you need to make in order to make people a priority in your life? What do you need to give up? What do you need to take on? No matter how high your career or business may take you, true success will be measured by how far you were able to reach down in order to lift up the people who helped you get there. Love is the greatest prize of all.

part 3

—⋘—

FINAL
THOUGHTS

Chapter 14

Promise or Compromise?

Voting in the 2018 Florida gubernatorial election had just finished, and I anxiously watched the results roll in while taxiing to the runway to fly to South America. The margins were razor thin, so thin that people knew there would be a runoff no matter who was declared the winner. Andrew Gillum took the early lead, but as more precincts reported results, Ron DeSantis overtook him. I switched my phone into airplane mode at takeoff, but *the moment* the flight attendant cleared her throat to announce we could use Wi-Fi, I was back online, refreshing my "live election results" browser every five minutes for the next four hours. By the time we landed in Guyana, Ron DeSantis was projected as the next governor of Florida.

I've always been politically amorphous. Purposely. I never publicly aligned myself with a political party, because with a career that included work at the local, state, and federal levels of government, spanning energy and environmental policy, juvenile justice policy, education policy, and appropriations, I *had* to be neutral. I needed to build and work with a broad coalition of legislators and advocates on *all* sides of my issues to advance them, so I never wanted to be pegged as a Democrat or Republican. I knew from watching others that once that happens, you're guaranteed to lose half the people you need. People had encouraged me to run for office a number of times, but a major part of what kept me from doing it was not wanting to place a stake in the ground, then getting mislabeled by others' preconceptions about what it means to have a *D* or an *R* beside your name.

I had voted across both sides of the aisle my entire life, paying more attention to a candidate's platform and track record than whether they were members of a particular party. And this had worked well for me in my legislative advocacy. I knew how to "code switch" depending on which legislator I was sitting in front of at the moment. If they were conservative and I was advocating for investing in juvenile delinquency prevention programs, it was about highlighting the cost of incarceration as opposed to prevention—a figure that was often two to three times as high, with higher recidivism and worse outcomes for society over time. If they were liberal and I was advocating for lessening regulatory requirements on carbon emissions, it was about the cost of upgrading power generation facilities that would be passed along to already impoverished customers and with minimal benefit to air quality. Since I didn't live in one party's echo chamber, I was able to interpret my issues across ideologies. I would get invitations to Democratic social events *and* Republican social events, and they both assumed I was on their team.

The week before Florida's gubernatorial election, I was wrapping up a meeting in New York when I saw my phone ring. I sent the call to voicemail and intended to check it later that evening, but the hustle and bustle of life made me forget. A couple of days later, while boarding a plane, I noticed the voicemail notification on my phone and remembered to check it. When I played the message, I heard, "Hi, Nona. This is Garrett, and I'm calling on behalf of the Andrew Gillum campaign. Listen, your name came up in a recent meeting, and I'd like to speak with you if you have a moment." I figured he was calling for a campaign contribution, but I thought it was odd since I wasn't a fixture in the Democratic party. I pressed "Call Back" as I settled into my seat on the plane, and he answered the phone on the second ring.

"Hi, Nona! Thanks for calling me back," Garrett said.

"Of course. Sorry it took me a little while. I'm either in meetings, on calls, or on planes most of the time, so I get a little behind, but I always call back," I said with a smile.

"No problem. Hey, listen. I'm working on the Gillum transition team, and as we head toward election day, we're putting together our short list for cabinet positions. Several people have recommended you for Secretary of the Department of Juvenile Justice, and I was just calling to see if you would be interested."

". . . I'm sorry. It's loud on this plane. I didn't hear you clearly. What did you say?"

"Oh, sure. I'm helping with the Gillum transition, and we're wanting to hit the ground running after the election. I just needed to know if you would be willing to be considered for Secretary of DJJ."

"Wow. I . . . I wasn't expecting this. At all. Umm. I'm hardly in the state and haven't been involved in government at any level since I joined Facebook. I'm honored to have been thought of. Umm. Okay, I guess you can put my name down."

"Awesome. Okay. I'll circle back with you after the

election. We'll need you to come to Tallahassee for some meetings after he wins. Have a great day."

I ended the call in a daze. What in the world was that? Where did that come from? How was my name mentioned when I'm not involved in state politics anymore? What does this mean? What did I just agree to? Thoughts raced through my mind like wildfire. I called my husband to tell him what had happened, and he was equally incredulous.

"Wait. What? They asked you to do what?"

"I know. I don't . . . I don't know."

"What would that require? I mean, you travel so much right now. Would it require more?"

"I have no idea. We didn't get into all that. I mean, it's just a preliminary conversation to gauge my willingness to be considered."

"Okay. Well, definitely keep me in the loop. That would be a major change for you. For our family."

"I know. And not something I ever considered or wanted either. Let's be praying for God's direction here."

A week later I was in South America when Ron DeSantis officially won the election, and I felt a personal sense of peace, knowing I no longer had to think about what a Cabinet Secretary role would require. When we returned from the trip to Greensboro, North Carolina, we decided to take a tour through the International Civil Rights Center and Museum before heading home. We were standing in the Woolworth counter exhibit when my phone rang with a call from an 850 area code.

"Who would be calling me from Tallahassee?" I thought before I answered the call. "Hi, this is Nona," I said.

"Hi, Nona. This is Ken. I'm calling on behalf of Governor-Elect Ron DeSantis's office. Your name was given to the Governor-Elect for Secretary of the Department of Juvenile Justice, and we were wondering if you could come to Tallahassee to meet with him and the Lieutenant Governor-Elect this Friday."

I stood in stunned silence.

"Hello? Nona? Are you there?"

"Um, yes. Yes, I'm here . . ."

"Would that work for you?"

"Well, I'm out of town for the rest of this week. I could make next Tuesday afternoon. Would that work?"

"Sure," Ken said. "How's two o'clock?"

"That works for me."

"Perfect. We'll see you then."

Tim happened to be looking at me when I took the call, and he kept staring at me as the color drained from my face. "What's wrong?" he asked.

"I don't know what just happened, but . . . I'm meeting with the Governor-Elect next week."

"The Governor-Elect? DeSantis? For what?"

"Yeah. He wants to talk about the Secretary of the Department of Juvenile Justice."

"Wait. Isn't that the same role the Gillum folks called you about?"

"Yes. Exact same role."

"Do you know DeSantis?"

"Not at all."

"How did they get your name?"

"I don't have a clue."

"Well, what are you going to do?"

"I . . . I guess I'm going to meet with him out of respect for his office. But I don't know that this is God's perfect will for me. We need to pray."

We drove back to our hotel in complete silence. We were both praying on the inside and wrestling with the incredible wrench that taking on such a role would throw into the trajectory I was on with Facebook. I didn't know God was about to teach me another lesson about faith.

———∞∞———

Success often means a plurality of opportunity. The more successful you are, the more doors will open for you. But I've learned in my life and career that not all *good* opportunities are God opportunities. It's critically important that we seek God for his will in our lives because without that anchor, we will drift into the open waters of our own desires.

Maybe you have a great singing voice, and God promised you would win the nations to his kingdom with it. But your desire to get "discovered" leads you to connect with a shady business manager who requires you to pay more than you can afford to get on stages that take you nowhere. Maybe you want to get married and God promised you a good, godly man, but your desire to join the "wives club" leads you to hook up with a guy who has been divorced twice and is still legally married to the third wife he's not yet divorced. Not very promising.

> Not all *good* opportunities are God opportunities.

In both cases, God promised to do something, but when presented with an opportunity that looked like the promise, you took matters into your own hands. Please understand that an opportunity that *looks* like God's promise is not the same thing as an opportunity that *is* God's promise. And no one demonstrates this better than the Father of Faith, Abraham.

In Genesis 15, God promised Abraham something that seemed impossible. He promised that Abraham would have a son despite being close to eighty years old. Not only that, but he promised that the number of Abraham's descendants would be as countless as the stars (verse 5). At this time, Abraham was elderly and had *zero* descendants, so the idea that he would have as many as the stars was a tall order. Yet the Bible says in verse 6, "Abram believed the LORD, and he credited it to him as righteousness." God spoke something unbelievable to Abraham, yet without flinching or batting an eye, Abraham believed God would do exactly what he said. This is one of the many reasons why God lauded Abraham's faith throughout the Bible. Because it didn't require convincing, argument, evidence, or demonstrations. Abraham took God at his word and trusted him. At least until another opportunity came his way.

With God's promise tucked away in his heart, Abraham was on the lookout for signs of Sarah's pregnancy. Months went by. Then a year. Then five years. Then ten years. Until, finally, in Genesis 16:1–2 we read, "Now Sarai, Abram's wife, had borne him no children. But she had an Egyptian slave named Hagar; so she said to Abram, 'The LORD has kept me from having children. Go, sleep with my slave; perhaps I can build a family through her.'"

Time for some straight talk. When this passage is taught from most pulpits, Sarah's suggestion that Abraham should rape and impregnate Hagar too often gets tempered and overlooked. Instead, what happened is usually framed as Abraham "lying" with Hagar. But this story is about forcing an innocent, powerless woman to birth a child against her will. And the consequence of this violence is reflected in the very nature of the child, Ishmael. The Bible says in Genesis 16:11–12,

The angel of the LORD also said to her:

> "You are now pregnant
>   and you will give birth to a son.
> You shall name him Ishmael,
>   for the LORD has heard of your misery.
> He will be a wild donkey of a man;
>   his hand will be against everyone
>   and everyone's hand against him,
> and he will live in hostility
>   toward all his brothers."

In other words, the child who was conceived in violence would bring violence wherever he went.

How could Abraham, whom God had credited as righteous, do such a thing? How could Sarah even *suggest* such a thing? I find the implications of this story to be both troubling and instructive. You see, eleven years had passed from the time God first promised Abraham a family to the birth of Ishmael. For those of us who are waiting on God for what he promised us, eleven *hours* can seem as if it is a long time. Eleven *days* can feel like an eternity. Eleven *months* can seem like an impossibility. Eleven *years*? If we aren't careful, the passage of time can have a way of wearing down our resolve to trust God. The first day God promises us something, we're hopeful and faithful. But as days turn to weeks turn to months turn to years and we have no evidence to point to the promise being fulfilled, we can begin to wonder whether the promise can be found around the corner. Whether we might bring it about in our own power. But as we see in the life of Abraham, when we force God's promise, we force a *com*promise and people get hurt. When our desire for success begins to have more power over our decision-making than our desire to honor God, poor decisions are sure to follow. And I'm no exception.

God told me that I wouldn't be at Facebook forever, so when the call came about joining the governor's cabinet, I immediately thought, "Lord, is this you calling me away from Facebook now? Is this what you meant?" I prayed about it earnestly in the days leading up to my meeting with the governor, trying to discern God's will with clarity and conviction. But I couldn't get clarity. Even after I met with the governor, I didn't feel settled in my spirit one way or the other, so I continued to go through the motions of the process while I prayed for God to help me sort everything out. I spoke with trusted friends, advisors, and mentors across the political spectrum to get their insight and input, but I still didn't feel peace. I remember one particular friend who pushed hard for me to take the job, citing that it would have made me the youngest person to serve at that level in the history of Florida. The more he talked about the perks of the job, the more my ego was stirred. And that's when I knew I needed godly counsel.

One of the most dangerous decision filters we can ever use is that of our ego. Ego looks at opportunities through the question: How will this benefit me? Humility evaluates opportunities through the question: How will this honor God? Once I felt my decision being led by my ego, I knew it was time to bring in someone who could reground me spiritually. I had been building a relationship with Bishop T. D. Jakes for a few months before getting the call and had spoken at his Woman Thou Art Loosed conference right before the opportunity arose, so I reached out to him and asked whether he would be willing to help me decipher

God's voice through the noise. He was on a plane, returning from out of the country, but said he would call me the moment he landed. Although much was said during the call, he regrounded me in humility by advising me to "never lose sight of your purpose. Every decision you make and every opportunity that comes your way should take you closer to your purpose."

If I had taken that job, I would have been required to stay landlocked in Tallahassee for the three-month legislative session that happens each year, beginning March in odd years and beginning in January in even years. The day after I spoke with Bishop Jakes, I got an email from Zondervan that said, "Great news! We're moving your book's birthday up from spring 2020 to January 2020!" The shift in release date would have directly conflicted with the 2020 legislative session because it would have started in January 2020, and the release of this book requires that I travel to promote it. Being part of the governor's cabinet would have required me to stay in Tallahassee, and being tied to one city for three months would have essentially put this book release at a standstill. In that, I heard God say no. My purpose in life is to bring hope to the hopeless through my story of God's faithfulness, and having to either run through the halls of the Florida legislature or fulfill that purpose through this book was a clear choice. What was indeed a good opportunity was not my *God* opportunity.

There may be some opportunities in your life that look like what God promised you, but they're actually a *com*-promise. Always remember that *likeness* is not the same as *authenticity*. You may know you've been called to the medical field, but you're thinking about majoring in business management because the school you're applying to is offering you more money if you choose business. You may know you're barely making ends meet right now, but a car salesman has been calling you with what seems to be a great deal on a new car. You may know that the vows you took to your spouse said you would be faithful to them for better or for worse, but you're in a season of "worse," and that man at the office who keeps asking to take you to lunch gave you a hug the other day that lingered. And you liked it. Hear me. Beware the *com*promise. If you continue reading the story of Abraham, you find that the lineages of Ishmael and Isaac birthed the nations of Palestine and Israel, nations that continue to be in conflict in the Middle East today.

We don't have the power to fulfill what God promised, even if what we force looks similar to what we *think* it should look like. Take heart in knowing that God is not slack about his promises. He is faithful to bring them to pass, so keep your choices rooted in God's eternal faithfulness.

Chapter 15

Failing Forward

In this final chapter, I want to discuss something that's very personal. I don't think a book about success would be complete if I didn't also discuss the role failure has played along the way. I shared a few examples in earlier chapters, but I want to focus on the one that has been most impactful for me. And it has nothing to do with my career. To "fail" means "to be unsuccessful in achieving one's goal" or "to neglect to do something." I have been successful in achieving my *professional* goals, but I realized a few years ago that the success of my career was overcrowding what was most important to me—my family. I share this with you as a cautionary tale so that you don't allow the pursuit of success to consume what matters most—the loved ones you get to do life with.

———— ∞∞∞ ————

"Mrs. Jones, can you do a parent-teacher conference this week?" asked my oldest son's first-grade teacher.

"Oh, I wish I could. I'm in Chicago through Friday. I'll

be home for a couple of days next Tuesday or Wednesday. Would that work?"

"Sure. Let's do Wednesday. See you then."

I knew what she wanted to talk about. My oldest son was six years old at the time and had been having some behavior issues in class. He and his brother were in a private school where behavior expectations were strictly enforced. He often came home with notes describing the things he did, such as talking back to his teacher, pushing a student at recess, or breaking a class rule by bringing a toy with him to school. I would FaceTime with him at the end of every day while I was away to ask how his day was, and I noticed he had become less and less talkative when I called. By the time my days ended, he was often long asleep, so there were times I was away that I would go days without speaking to him. When I was able to block time in my day to call him before bed, there were a few times when he said he didn't want to speak to me. And it hurt.

I knew something was going on, and given my own experience as a child, I asked him what had happened to make him so angry. He would shrug his shoulders, say, "I don't know," and go back to doing whatever he was doing.

"Thanks for meeting with me, Mrs. Jones," said his teacher. "I want to start by saying your son is brilliant. He learns everything quickly and does so well on his schoolwork. But his behavior has gotten out of control."

"I know," I said. "And I'm really sorry about that. His father and I are working on it. I travel a lot for work, so I'm doing the best I can when I'm home."

She paused. "That's what I wanted to talk with you about. I recently kept him in the classroom during recess because he had behaved so badly that morning, and I noticed that he was crying at his desk. When I asked him what was wrong, he said he missed you. He said you're never home, and that's why he's so angry all the time."

My heart shattered. Tears formed in my eyes. In all my diagnosing what could be causing my son to act out, it never occurred to me that *I* was the reason. In my hustle to succeed at my career, I had failed as a mother because I had neglected the most important thing in the world to me. My son. I'd had a very full work and travel schedule since stepping into my first executive role, but before I had children, my husband and I were able to manage my being gone for a day or two here and there just fine. After I had children, despite having two human beings who were entirely dependent on me, I had never adjusted my schedule to make room for them.

In many ways, my life was out of sync with the lives of my colleagues. Many of them weren't married or didn't have children, and the ones who *did* have children had adult children. For them, life was lived freely without concerns about picking anyone up from daycare, cooking dinner, scheduling well-child checkups around offsite strategy meetings, or juggling the random days when school would be closed while work was open. I will never forget the Thursday when someone pinged me to ask whether I could attend a meeting in London the following Monday. They didn't have children and weren't married, so for them, it was as simple as taking a drive to the grocery store. But for me, there were logistical issues that required weeks of planning. The downside of achieving success at an early age is that you tend to either postpone the demands of family life to manage the success, or you end up neglecting the demands of family life to manage success. I didn't like either of those options, so I decided to chart my own way.

I picked up my phone the next morning and called my executive assistant, Janice.

"Janice, we need to go through my calendar and list out every future trip that doesn't require me to be there. Things like a conference I'm not speaking at, a meeting I'm not a decision-maker at, and anything I agreed to attend only because someone asked me to. I need to strip my calendar down to the essentials. Nothing more."

"Yes, ma'am," said Janice.

By the time she prepared the list of "nonessential travel," I could see full days of time I could take back. I also realized that a lot of what I had on my calendar had nothing to do with me and everything to do with pleasing other people. A good 40 percent of my calendar was commitments I made because I didn't want to disappoint someone, but when faced with the choice between disappointing them and disappointing my child, they were going to lose every time.

As if God was testing my newfound resolve, my boss emailed to ask me to attend a conference happening two weeks later in Washington, DC.

"Thank you so much for thinking of me. I'm unable to attend due to family commitments at that time," I replied.

I didn't have an "event" on my calendar. But I *did* have my son on my heart. Later that afternoon, I picked him up from school and asked to speak with him. I gave my younger son a snack and headed upstairs with my oldest.

"Do you know I love you?" I asked.

He shook his head no as he looked at the floor.

I gently cupped his chubby little face with my hands and lifted it until his eyes met mine.

"Baby boy, Mommy has failed you. I've been putting my job and everyone else ahead of you, and for that, I'm sorry. Nothing in this world means more to me than you."

His little eyes filled with tears, making mine fill with tears too.

"Listen, from now on I can promise you that if I have to leave, it will be because it's absolutely essential for my work, okay?"

"Okay," he said through tears.

"And I want you and me to have a mommy-son day this weekend. Just the two of us, okay?"

His eyes twinkled and he smiled. "Really? Just me and you?"

"Yep! Just me and you. Would that work with your schedule?" I asked jokingly.

"I'll make it work," he responded with a laugh.

That weekend, my little boy and I went to the beach. I left my work phone at home and kept my personal phone on silent so I could focus entirely on him. We had a great time riding go-karts, playing putt-putt golf, and eating pizza. When the weekend came to a close, we prayed together that God would always keep us close. That was a few years ago, and things haven't always been perfect, but as he sits next to me in bed while I write this final chapter, it's a physical reminder that no matter how badly we mess up, we always have the opportunity to redeem our failures by learning from them, changing from them, and growing from them. There will be times when you will miss the mark of a goal you set for yourself, but keep the bigger picture in mind. To *fail* is not to be a *failure*. To fail is simply to learn a new way not to do something.

After we have failed, we will find ourselves at a crossroads. We will have to choose what to do with the broken pieces of the goal we set for ourselves. Your past pain may have equipped you only to surrender when you fail, to wallow in the

> To fail is simply to learn a new way not to do something.

discouragement and guilt of missing the mark. But I want to encourage you to know that the best of us are simply people who have learned how to give the fragments of failure to God and allowed him to rebuild us as he sees us. Jeremiah 29:11 says, "'For I know the plans I have for you,' declares the LORD, 'plans to prosper you and not to harm you, plans to give you hope and a future.'" In the hands of God, the broken pieces of past failure can pave the pathway to better decisions *next time*. You have a future. You have hope. The beauty of God is that he never discards us just because we made a mess of things. Instead, when we made the biggest mess in the universe, he peered down from heaven, then leaned over to Jesus and said, "Only you can clean that up."

In Christ we have the grace to start over again, starting from the inside out.

Epilogue

Succeeding after Surviving

Now that you've read this book, I want to leave you with a final word of encouragement. Fixing what's broken requires the right tool, so the ideas I've offered to you are simply a few tools for your tool kit. My hope is that a few of these ideas, when put into practice, will help you push through the emotional, mental, and spiritual roadblocks that have kept you from reaching your best and highest potential in life. Everything I've shared is born out of my own life and experience, so I'm not offering you theories or hypotheses. I'm offering you my truth.

People have said I'm brave to tell my story with such transparency, but I don't see it that way. Bravery requires mustering the courage to do something you would rather not do if given the chance, but there is nothing I would rather do than help you see that you aren't alone in your struggles. No matter what it may look like on the outside, we are all fighting a private battle at any given moment. But I want you to know that the battle you are fighting has already been won. The victory was won by Jesus on our

215

behalf long ago. You are not fighting *for* victory. Instead, you are fighting *from* victory.

When lauded for the number of slaves Harriet Tubman freed through the Underground Railroad, she didn't celebrate. Instead, she lamented, saying, "I could have freed more if only they had realized they were slaves." The first step you may need to take is admitting that the past isn't the past. The past is your present. A hurt you've been trying hard to ignore continues to shape the way you think, how you feel, and what you do. But ignoring it doesn't make it go away. Success isn't elusive for you. It's as close as the choice to do the hard work needed to get free from the past in order to build a fulfilling future.

Success begins within.

If a girl like me, whose past should have voided her future, can do it, I know that through the redeeming power of Christ, you can do it too. Success begins within.

Acknowledgments

My deepest admiration and thanks go to my husband, Tim. You have been a partner with me through so much of what I shared in this book, and although it wasn't easy, we have pressed our way through it, and our love is stronger than it has ever been. My greatest success in this life is being your wife and TJ and Isaac's mommy. I love you, and thank you for loving me.

A major thank-you to my Aunt Gwen (i.e., Brenda), who not only helped ensure that my reconstruction of family events was accurate, but who has also been my biggest cheerleader, next to my husband, for everything I have done. Thank you for the stories about my dad that made me laugh, made me cry, and made me grateful. And I especially want to thank you for being the mother I always wanted. My boys love you like their grandmother because that is what you have been to them.

I had no plans to write this book. I didn't have and still don't have a literary agent. I wasn't shopping a manuscript around in hopes of getting a book deal. And yet here I am. I give all honor, glory, and gratitude to God for orchestrating the means by which this book made it into your hands, because it had absolutely nothing to do with me.

It was the summer of 2018 when I was speaking with a friend about the subject I planned to speak on at Bishop Jakes's Woman Thou Art Loosed conference that October, and he said, "You need to write that in a book." I laughed at the suggestion, but he said, "I'm serious. That's a message people need to hear. You need to write that in a book." After hanging up with him, I thought about it and figured it wouldn't hurt to try, so I started working on the manuscript in an effort to have something available at the conference. I had no idea that as soon as I finished the manuscript, I would be invited to submit it to Zondervan for review. It was the divine encouragement of my friend Johnny Stephens that brought this work to be. Thank you, Johnny, for seeing in me what I didn't see and encouraging me to do what I would have never done without you planting the seed. I appreciate you.

I cannot overstate how incredible the Zondervan team is. Tom Dean, thank you for being my personal champion and seeing something in my manuscript that made you put your full support behind it. Stephanie Smith, not only are you an incredible editor who deeply understood my message, but you also have the gift of encouragement and spoke life over me when I needed it most (and you didn't even know it). Robin Barnett, I'm so grateful for your enthusiasm about bringing this message to the masses and understanding my passion for building a bridge across faith, business, and trauma. It's not an easy task, but you understood what that would require and dove in head first with me. Kim Tanner, having your eyes on my final edited manuscript was gold. You continued to chisel away at my story until what remained for the world to read was the best it could possibly be. Your thoughtful questions, edits, and comments made me feel like you really cared about this book, and I will always cherish them. David Morris, thank you for your support and enthusiasm about this book. Knowing that you have been cheering me on throughout this process has been a blessing of immense proportions.

To my superhero of a writing coach, Margot Starbuck, thank you for pushing me to write a book that was deeper and wider than what I could have ever imagined. The manuscript I turned in and the book people now read are two completely different works, thanks to you. I appreciate every time you challenged me to expand a thought, to clarify, to provide examples, and to involve the reader. I loved having you mark up my chapters with your comments, critiques, and jokes because you truly got me, and that mattered so much. Your sense of humor and ability to capture voice is unparalleled. You have made me a better writer.

To my friend and mentor, Christine Caine, thank you for being willing to lend your voice to my story. I have learned so much from you about resilience, purpose, humility, and faithfulness, and it is my honor to have you on this journey with me. I must also thank Karol Mason for being an integral part of my life and professional journey. You are, undoubtedly, the best example of what *good* success looks like. You carry your influence with grace, dignity, intellect, and confidence, and I want to be like you when I grow up. To Lorraine Brock and Jane Adams, thank you for taking me under your wing when I needed professional perspective and advocates in the rooms I wasn't in.

To Mrs. Johnson, my fourth-grade teacher who pulled me to the side one day and said, "Nona, you're capable of better." Thank you for planting that seed in my heart when the soil was hardened through pain and disappointment.

I've never forgotten that, even when my behavior didn't immediately show it. A major thank-you to my sixth-grade teachers who determined I was capable of more and made me see my own potential when I didn't think there was any there. And to Pastor Larry and Sister Susan, thank you so much for your love, support, and encouragement. To this day.

To my many friends and supporters who purchased this book before it was even released, I cannot thank you enough for your faith in me. You have no idea how much your gesture kept me going as we made our way to this day. You didn't have to do it, but you did. And I am grateful to all of you.

Notes

Chapter 1: Surviving Isn't Enough

1. Brené Brown, "Listening to Shame," TED Talk, March 16, 2012, https://youtu.be/psN1DORYYV0.

Chapter 3: Releasing the Why

1. Viktor Frankl, *Man's Search for Meaning* (Boston: Beacon, 1946), Kindle edition.

Chapter 4: Choosing Freedom

1. Anthony Ray Hinton and Lara Love Hardin, *The Sun Does Shine: How I Found Life and Freedom on Death Row* (New York: St. Martin's, 2018), 98.
2. Anthony Ray Hinton, "How I Got 30 Years on Death Row for Someone Else's Crime," April 27, 2018, *The Guardian*, https://www.theguardian.com/us-news/2018/apr/27/anthony-ray-hinton-death-row-a-legal-lynching-alabama-crime.

Chapter 5: Never beyond Repair

1. Julie Unruh, "Human Trafficking Victim Using Past to Help Others—But Needs to Clear Her Name," WGNTV, July 20, 2017, https://wgntv.com/2017/07/20/human-trafficking-victim-using-past-to-help-others-but-needs-help-to-clear-her-name/.
2. Ibid.

Chapter 6: Run Your Own Race

1. Bishop T. D. Jakes, Woman Thou Art Loosed Master Class, October 2018.

Chapter 7: Success versus *Good* Success

1. Verna Noel Jones, "A New Life after TIA," *StrokeSmart*, August 23, 2007, https://www.strokesmart.org/article?id=255.
2. Ibid.

Success On Purpose

1. https://www.dictionary.com/browse/purpose.

Chapter 8: Build Gratitude

1. Sheryl Sandberg, *Option B: Facing Adversity, Building Resilience, and Finding Joy* (New York: Knopf, 2017), 6.
2. Ibid., 32.
3. Faith and Technology, *Praise*, TBN, 2019.

Chapter 9: Build Character

1. "Halle Berry on Eric Benét Cheating," *The Oprah Winfrey Show*, 2004.
2. "Eric Benét's Confessions," *People*, July 11, 2005, https://people.com/archive/eric-benets-confessions-vol-64-no-2/.

Chapter 11: Build Curiosity

1. "Bill Gates," *The David Rubenstein Show*, October 17, 2016, https://www.bloomberg.com/news/videos/2016-10-17/the-david-rubenstein-show-bill-gates.

Chapter 13: Build Love for People

1. Valerie Rice, "Unrecognized Apple II Employees Exit," *InfoWorld*, April 15, 1985.
2. Ibid.